Giza Occasional Papers 1

Giza Plateau Mapping Project
Season 2004
Preliminary Report

Giza Occasional Papers 1

Giza Plateau Mapping Project
Season 2004
Preliminary Report

Mark Lehner, Mohsen Kamel, and Ana Tavares

Ancient Egypt Research Associates, Inc.

Published by Ancient Egypt Research Associates, Inc.
26 Lincoln Street, Suite 5, Boston, MA 02135 USA

Ancient Egypt Research Associates (AERA) is a 501(c) (3), tax-exempt, nonprofit organization dedicated to research on ancient Egypt at the Giza Plateau.

Layout and editing by Alexandra Witsell and Wilma Wetterstrom.

Printed in Hollis, New Hampshire, by Puritan Press.

ISBN: 0-9779370-6-2

Cover photo: The Eastern Town House (ETH), excavations in progress, looking northwest. The ETH is discussed on pages 16–18. Photo by Mark Lehner.

Contents

Preface

We began our Giza Occasional Papers (GOP) series with the publication of a lengthy summary of the Giza Plateau Mapping Project (GPMP) 2005 season, and we called it GOP2 with the intention of backtracking to publish the summary of our 2004 season as GOP1, which we now present.

The delay between writing these summaries at the end of a field season and publishing them online or in print means that at the time of publication we actually know more about excavation areas or topics where we have continued in a subsequent field season. Nevertheless, I believe it is useful to publish these reports and the site maps that accompany them as we wrote and prepared them at the time, rather than trying too much to update them to reflect real-time understandings, because one of the purposes of our GOP series is to show the evolution of our knowledge from one season to another, as well as to simply get out the information in preliminary form.

I emphasize the preliminary nature of the GOP monographs. Since 2004 it has been the practice of GPMP archaeologists who serve as Area Supervisors to prepare at the end of a season a Data Structure Report (DSR), which is the technical excavation report, containing a narrative of the excavation procedure and methods, a phasing of the principal periods represented by stratigraphic features (depositional units and cuts), a matrix of the chronological relationships of those features, and all lists including those of features, drawings, photographs, and samples. The DSRs are the primary data of our excavations. Authors will write final reports on the basis of the DSR and its site phasing, combined with input from material culture analysts and their reports.

The GOP monographs are more general descriptive reports, by the project and field directors, sometimes with summaries contributed by the Area Supervisors. They are preliminary reports in which we intend to present a general description of the results of field seasons—archaeological tableaus present at the end of excavations—and working hypotheses about these results.

Mark Lehner

Acknowledgements

For a very successful season, and for collaboration based in deep friendship, I am grateful to Dr. Zahi Hawass, Undersecretary of State and Secretary General of the Supreme Council of Antiquities (SCA). We thank Sabry Abd al-Aziz, General Director of Pharaonic Monuments; Atef Abu Dahab, Director of Giza and Saqqara; and Adel Hussein, Director of Giza. We enjoyed working in close collaboration with Mansour Boraik, Chief Inspector of Giza, and Inspector Mohammed Shiha, who represented the SCA during our 2004 season. We thank Mohammed Hameda who also represented the SCA with our team, and the following inspectors: Shiama Mohammed, Fatma Hussein, Heba Hosni, and Amira Hassan, who represented the SCA and who worked with us at the excavation site. We would like to thank Ahmed Eiz who served as our inspector in the storeroom. We are especially grateful to Engineer Abd al-Hamid Kotb for assistance with mechanized equipment for clearing modern overburden from our site so that we could carry out the archaeology. Once again this season we are grateful for the services of loader operator, Mohammed Musilhi, who carried out this task with skill and determination. Without this help we could not have carried out the work summarized here. Reis Ahmed Abd al-Basat did a remarkable job supervising our specialist workers and skilled excavators from Luxor.

Ann Lurie, on behalf of the Ann and Robert H. Lurie Foundation, once again insured that our goals for a long, ambitious, and rewarding season 2004 were fully met, and for this we offer special thanks. We also offer special thanks to David H. Koch, Peter Norton, and Nathan Myrhvold for major support. I am grateful to Bruce Ludwig who has helped to develop financial support for our work at Giza since 1986. Our 2004 season would not have been possible without the support of Jon Jerde, Robert Lowdermilk, Glen Dash, Matthew McCauley, George Link, James Allen, Douglas Rawles, Ann Thompson, Bill and Kathy Dahlmal, Fred and Suzanne Rheinstein, Sandford and Betty Sigoloff, Victor and Nancy Moss, David Goodman, Marjorie Fisher, Alice Hyman, Don Kunz, Bonnie Sampsell, Lora Lehner, and Craig Smith. And we welcome the support of Michael Fourticq, George Sherman, Michael K. MacDonald, Donna L. Dinardo, Robin Young, and Barbara Russo.

Mark Lehner

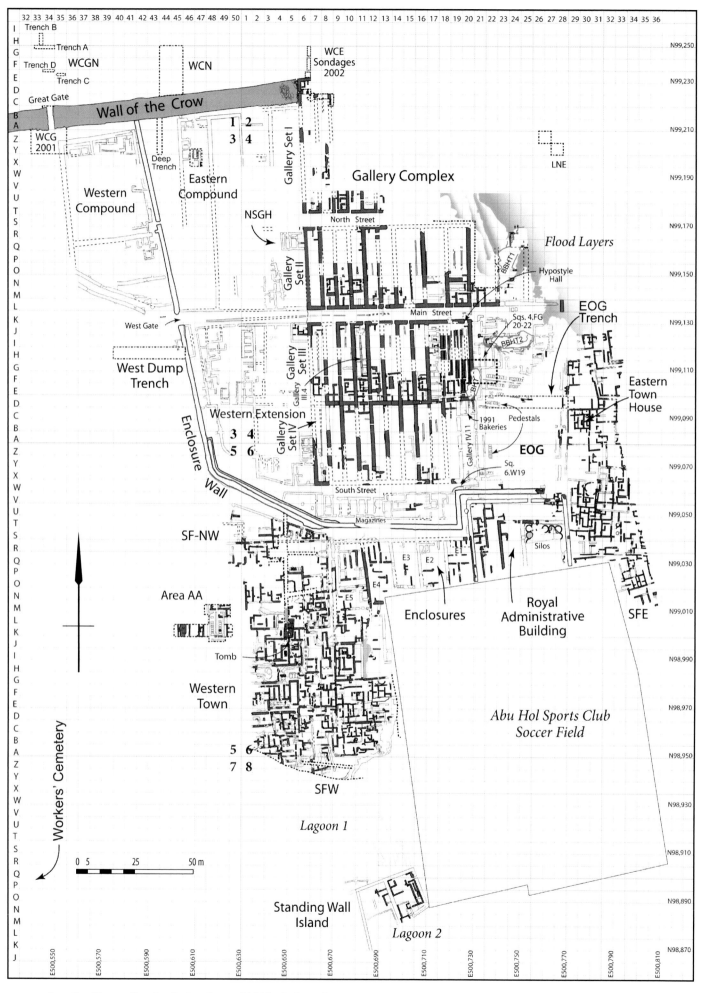

1. Introduction

Our 2004 field season began on January 8, 2004, and drew to a close on May 31, 2004.

It was AERA's first major season of the GPMP after our 2003 "study season," which was a break after our Millennium Project—three years (1999–2002) of intensive clearing, mapping, and excavation of the ruins of the site called *Heit el-Ghurob* (HeG), Arabic for "Wall of the Crow," a local name for this tract of ground after its most defining feature, the 200-m-long stone wall on the northwest of the site (fig. 1). The 2004 season was in a sense the final push of our Millennium Project, because we added to the map of the "Lost City of the Pyramids" site the Western Town, a major component of the overall settlement consisting of a series of large house-like structures.

In 2003 we established some of our report-writing protocols. We hope that in the years that follow, we will further publish a series of both preliminary reports in GOPs like this one, and more developed presentations in our Giza Reports series, as we carry on with our investigations into ancient settlements at the foot of the Giza Pyramids Plateau.

Review of Clearing and Excavation Procedures

Since 1999 our excavation seasons have included large scale clearing of a sandy overburden and mapping of the ruins of an underlying ancient settlement over broad areas, as well as intensive, detailed excavations of selected, specific parts of the site.

Broad Area Clearing and Mapping
In our large scale clearing we removed a thick overburden of sandy material deposited on the site in recent times, some trash, but mostly sand mixed with chaff and straw from cleaning the riding stables in Nazlet es-Semman and Kafr Gebel, modern excavation dumps, and some underlying clean sand.

Wind deposited the clean sand already in ancient times, but each day, until the last few years, sand diggers from the nearby riding stables would take clean sand from this site to the riding stables where it is spread on the floor to absorb camel, donkey, and, mostly, horse droppings. The stables are cleaned on a daily basis and the sand diggers would bring the sand with its new inclusions back to the site where they would dump it and take fresh clean sand. In this way they turned over much of the clean sand layer across the site.

Below the modern deposits and whatever clean sand is left, we find the surface of the ruins of a large Old Kingdom settlement. Before wind deposited the blanket of clean sand over this surface, forces of erosion cut the settlement ruins at waist to ankle level and blew the material away. This left a horizontal section through the ancient settlement, and we can see and map ancient walls of mudbrick and fieldstone without excavating, or with just shallow excavation, surface scraping, or even with light cleaning.

Detailed Excavation
We excavate intensively in smaller areas. When we excavate, we assign feature numbers to layers, floors, postholes, hearths, and walls. Feature numbers are checked out as needed from a feature log, so that the numbers never repeat across the site. For each feature we fill out an information form, write narrative notes, and do photographs, maps, and section drawings. The area, square number, and feature number are included on all material saved from the excavation and sent to the storeroom. We number the bags in which we send material up to the storeroom and lab, whether the "bag" is a film canister with charcoal or a 15-kilogram sandbag of pottery. When we excavate through the decayed mudbrick and other compact sediments to the living floors of that period, we save and count or weigh all material culture—all chipped stone, pottery, seal impressions, charcoal, and stone, such as granite and alabaster exotic to Giza. We take samples of sediments for the flotation process to recover charred plant remains. We dry sieve the sediments on site and wet sieve the finer material in the storeroom to recover the smallest animal bone, chipped stone, pottery, and seal impressions.

Figure 1. Facing page, plan of the Heit el-Ghurob site showing the 2004 and previous operations.

Major Clearing and Excavation Areas of 2004

We carried out large-scale clearing during the 2004 season focused in two major areas:

1. Around the soccer field
2. North of the Wall of the Crow

We carried out detailed excavations in the following places:

1. West Dump (WD)
2. North Street Gate House (NSGH)
3. East of the Galleries (EOG)
4. Faience Working Area (part of EOG)
5. Eastern Town House (ETH)
6. Royal Administrative Building (RAB)
7. West of the soccer field (SFW)
8. North of the Gate in the Wall of the Crow (WCGN)

In this report we will first discuss the detailed excavations in areas we cleared in earlier seasons. Then we will discuss the areas newly cleared and excavated this season.

Figure 2. Adel Kelany maps layers running to the Enclosure Wall in a deep probe in the West Dump trench (WD).

2. 2004 Excavation in Previously Cleared Areas

West Dump

Since the beginning of our excavations in 1988–'89, we have seen indications that the ancient inhabitants of the site might have dumped waste on the slopes west of the Enclosure Wall. Main Street of the Gallery Complex opens through the Enclosure Wall at West Gate. It was our hypothesis that the inhabitants of the galleries and the Western Extension carried waste out this gate and dumped it on the western slope.

Area WD ("West Dump") is on the slope of the plateau leading up to the Workers' Cemetery. The tombs of the lower parts of that cemetery appear to sit upon part of this dump. In their excavations of the lower cemetery, the archaeologists working under Dr. Hawass broke through the dump layers at one small spot. Immediately, they turned up copper bits, flint blades, and quantities of pottery.

Goals for Area WD

Excavations in these dumps might give us information about everyday life within the galleries. Another goal was to ascertain the stratigraphic (chronological) relationships between the slope, which the Workers' Cemetery occupies farther south, and the Workers' City on the low desert below. For these reasons we planned an east-west trench along the western slope outside the Gallery Complex not far south of West Gate.

Lauren Bruning and Adel Kelany supervised excavation in a 30-m excavation trench spaced in the H-tier of Grid 3, down the western slope, dropping 2.5 m from the top of the operation to the Enclosure Wall just south of West Gate opening to Main Street (figs. 1, 2).

WD Results Upslope

Gray, sherd-rich, ashy rubble was exposed at the high end of the trench. We thought that this material was part of a considerable dump up against the western slope. But Bruning and Kelany found that here the ancient trashy deposit (feature [20,799]) is only 60 to 70 cm thick. Moreover, this layer has been severely pitted and turned over, leaving interspersed sandy layers. They found some

human bone within these ashy layers, probably from disturbed Late Period burials. Johnny Karlsson excavated two Late Period burials that were more intact. Bruning and Kelany recovered Old Kingdom pottery sherds with copper adhering and a copper crucible from the dump layers.

The trash layers lie upon a deposit of concentrated limestone chips. This material turned out to be artificial, not just scree of local limestone washed down off the Maadi Formation slope. The concentrated limestone chips slope down to the east. The limestone fragments are irregular—but not with sharp edges as we have seen in some ancient stone-working deposits.

Within this mass we could discern a rectangle of more consolidated, larger limestone fragments flanked north and south by channels, about 20 cm wide, filled with finer material. A wider channel on the east is about 40 cm wide.

We seem to have here at least one of the crude pedestals of the kind so ubiquitous in Area EOG and of a finer variety in our 1988–'89 building in Area AA (Lehner 2002). It is odd that they should occur here at the break of the western slope. Ideally we would have cleared a 5 × 5-m square of the overlying dump layer to see if more of these structures exist at this location. However, Jessica Kaiser, our osteo-archaeologist, estimated that we would have to excavate at least nine more Late Period burials sunk into the dump and underlying stony layer. For this reason we did not excavate the stony features further in favor of other priorities.

WD Results Downslope

At the bottom of the slope, Bruning and Kelany surveyed an extension of the trench, 7 m long and 2 m wide, up to the Enclosure Wall.

Exposure of the Enclosure Wall

The eastern end of the trench exposed the Enclosure Wall for a height of 1 m. The wall appears to have been built in two stages, a lower one, 40 to 43 cm thick, of white limestone pieces in a gray mud matrix, and an upper one, 50 to 60 cm thick, of more yellowish limestone in a mud matrix. These stages could be merely two courses of the same construction period. However, the top of a layer [20,788] of concentrated sherds, 24 cm thick, runs up to the wall just at the interface of the upper and lower phase, suggesting the upper phase was added when the surface had risen. The lower phase of the Enclosure Wall was founded here upon a layer of gritty, tan sand [20,805], 9 to 12 cm thick, which includes a patch of crushed limestone [20,804].

Stratigraphy at the Enclosure Wall

There is no obvious roadbed outside of, and along, the Enclosure Wall.

The people who occupied the site left a sequence of layers rich in pottery sherds and other material that abutted against the Enclosure Wall. They left the lowest of these layers [20,801] shortly after they built the Enclosure Wall around elevation 16.64 above sea level (asl) upon successive layers of limestone rubble [20,803], crushed limestone [20,804], and more rubble [20,805].

The layer [20,805] upon which the inhabitants built the Enclosure Wall stretches 7 m to the west. Under the Enclosure Wall, Bruning and Kelany found a sandy layer [20,808] with limestone fragments, marl brick debris, frequent pottery sherds, and animal bones.

They excavated deeper in a 1 × 1.2-m probe in the southeast corner of Square 3.H45, 2 m west of the Enclosure Wall, down to a depth of 2.22 m from the ground surface. They found another layer [20,811], 50 cm thick, of laminated sand with frequent pottery sherds and animal bones, charcoal, and some chipped flint. This material decreased deeper into the probe. Next came relatively clean sand [20,812], 44 cm thick, followed by a lens of moist, dark soil with pottery fragments [20,814], 7 to 10 cm thick. Finally the wd probe went through a layer of largely sterile sand [20,815], 53 cm deeper. It had no cultural material, except for one flint pebble.

The section balks of the 1 × 2-m probe now stood 1.20 m high. The probe had reached 15.22 m asl, about 80 cm lower than the level of the nearby Main Street, 30 cm lower than the latest floors in Gallery III.4, 1.08 m lower than the compact Old Kingdom surface north of the Gate in the Wall of the Crow, and 35 cm higher than the earliest occupation found (at 14.88 m asl) under Gallery I.3 in the deep probe in Area wce.

Kelany excavated the deep probe to a depth of 2.90 m from the surface, until he hit the water table at elevation 14.66 m asl, 10 cm deeper than the ground water in Lagoon 1 alongside the soccer field, and 10 cm higher than the water table in Trench A in wcgn. The material at this depth is relatively clean sand [20,815], but still with the occasional alluvial mud and pottery sherd, indicating the presence of people. Note that the bottom of Kelany's probe is 22 cm lower than the bottom of the deep probe in wce, at 14.88 m asl.

Kelany did two more trenches (c and d) in Area wd to link up Trench b on the "West Dump" slope with Trench a against the Enclosure Wall. He found more of the same or similar sandy layers—[20,823] in Trench c and [20,826] in Trench d—with much cultural material, charcoal, ash, and pottery sherds. The material appeared to have been washed by water.

Older Fieldstone Wall

Stones protruding from the north section of the deep probe belong to a deeper, older wall that had been hiding just behind the face of the section. The older wall is about 1.07 m below the surface, 2.15 m west of, and just a little lower than, the bottom of the Enclosure Wall. (Layers [20,803], [20,804], and [20,805] intervene between the older and younger walls.) The lower wall is built upon a few centimeters of sand [20,812] just above a layer of many pottery fragments [20,814]. The wall [20,839] measures 1.45 m wide east-west and 50 cm high. The wall is wider at the bottom than at the top (as preserved, the wall once rose higher). The eastern face of this wall is plastered with mud. It appears to be a true end, not a corner or a wall that had been cut through.

It was surprising and coincidental enough that a wall had been hidden just behind the sand in the north cut of the trench. But then, on the very day we were back-filling the trench near the end of the season, the remains of another wall announced itself in the southern face of Trench a! When the south section collapsed we saw three limestone blocks at the same level as the wall [20,839] in the north section. The blocks have no mortar but they line up, 1.10 m wide and 17 cm high. The blocks appear to belong to the butt end of another fieldstone wall.

The distance between these blocks and the wall [20,839] in the north section is 1.80 m. The two wall ends appear to form a gate. The walls run somewhat north-south like the Enclosure Wall (actually west of north, east of south). Perhaps this is an earlier version of West Gate at the far west end of Main Street, albeit slightly farther south.

North Street Gate House (NSGH)

Our work in North Street Gate House continued excavations started in 2001–'02 (fig. 3). In previous seasons Mohsen Kamel supervised excavations in North Street Gate House (nsgh). We have dubbed this building a "gate house" because it sits just south of the entrance of North Street into the Gallery Complex, between Gallery Sets i and ii.

Figure 3. Overview of the NSGH. The bakery can be seen in the foreground on the right. View to the northwest.

Late Period Burials at NSGH

Many Late Period Burials complicated the task of excavating NSGH. Osteo-archaeologists Jessica Kaiser, Johnny Karlsson, and Tove Björk documented, mapped, and removed 46 burial cuts. Three of the burial pits had no human remains. The rest varied in sex and age, ranging from children to adults. Apart from occasional coffin fragments, few burial objects were included with the skeletons. The exceptions were amulets with some of the child burials and some pottery with two of the adult burials. A child burial included a cache of cowry shells and a large sacred eye amulet. The remains of a faience bead net dress accompanied the skeletal remains of a young woman of 12 to 16 years. Orientation of the burials was primarily east-west with some minor variation from the true axis. (See Kaiser 2005 for further details on the Late Period burials and cemetery itself.)

The Old Kingdom Layout of NSGH

Ann Foster (2004) supervised the excavation of the Old Kingdom deposits.

North Street Gate House has a five-room core (Rooms 4, 5, 6, 7 and Vestibule 2) entered by a little ramp up to a narrow doorway (62 cm wide) on the northeast against the west wall of Gallery Set II, which is also the east wall of

NSGH (fig. 4). The doorway through the 1.50-m thickness of the southern wall of North Street led into Vestibule 1.

Entering Vestibule 1, an immediate right turn put one in Room 3 which is a magazine corridor leading to Vestibule 4 (see below). If you did not turn into Room 3, you could enter straight into Vestibule 2, misnamed because it is actually one of the largest rooms in the house, about 2 m wide and more than 3 m long (north-south). Vestibule 2 gave access to Rooms 4, 6, and 7.

A narrow doorway in the southern wall of Vestibule 2 opens into the small Room 7, 2.3 × 1 m. Late Period burials badly disturbed the floors and deposits. There remain traces of a plastered shelf along the inside of the northern wall. We hypothesized Room 7 might be for sleeping because of the raised floor level and offset doorway.

A doorway in the west wall of Vestibule 2 puts you in Room 6, about 2.2 × 3.10 m, about the same size as Vestibule 2. Late Period burials destroyed about half the floor deposits, but enough remained to ascertain that at one time the inhabitants used Room 6 as a bakery (fig. 3). Below an ash deposit, two shallow worn ditches ran parallel to the western and eastern walls. These appear to be baking pits, and smaller depressions within the ditches were probably bread mold sockets. Two large, shallow pits in the southwestern corner are probably emplacements

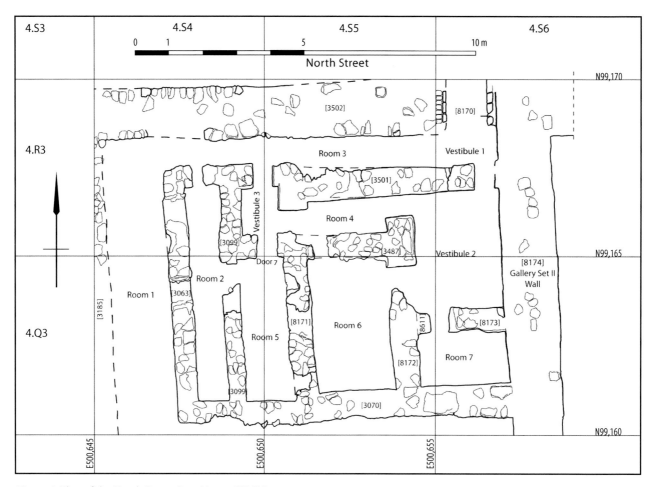

Figure 4. Plan of the North Street Gate House (NSGH).

for vats, and we might understand a crude, stony hearth platform in the northwest corner as the spot where the bread molds were stack-heated, as shown in Old Kingdom tomb scenes and figurines.

On the basis of the size and location of North Street Gate House, and on the basis of material culture from pre-2004 excavations, we have hypothesized that the occupants were of higher status than people in the galleries. We need to assess this idea against the fact that, during at least one period, the largest central room of the house was given over to bread-baking in open pits (so probably left unroofed). Or is this a secondary, later, function of this room?

A right turn in Vestibule 1 gives access to a corridor (Room 3) running west along the north side of the house. The corridor contained storage jars and bread molds resting in place against the north wall. The corridor leads to two doorways on the left (south). The first doorway opens access to a small foyer (Vestibule 3) from which doorways opened east to Room 4, or south to Room 5.

Room 4, 1.05 m (2 cubits) wide and 3.75 m long, is another east-west corridor or magazine that was also

entered from Vestibule 2 through a doorway on the east only 66 cm wide.

In Room 5 Foster traced a floor [2600] south from Vestibule 3 through Door 7 to the south wall of NSGH. She "associated a single ash deposit [2612] resting against the east wall of the room [8171] and on the floor [2600], with burn marks on the wall and posits a small hearth here. Three other burn marks on the walls—in the south corners of the room as well as across the room from [2612] on the western wall [3099]—were also noted, though no associated ash deposit was found in association with the southeast corner mark" (Foster 2004: 9).

If Room 5 was the main living room, it might be surprising to have it separated from Room 7—if Room 7 was for sleeping—by an open-air bakery, that is, if the bakery function of Room 6 is contemporary with floor [2600].

The second doorway at the western end of the corridor (Room 3) opened to a magazine (Room 2), 5 m long and only 90 cm wide oriented north-south, and lying west of the core house (fig. 5). Fine red, "Meidum ware" bowls, a jar stand, bread molds, and a beer jar were *in situ* on

Figure 5. Pots stored in a magazine (Room 2) in the North Street Gate House (NSGH).

the floor of this magazine. Foster (2004: 5) wrote that the ceramic deposit "was primarily composed of large fragments of nearly intact storage jars and associated contents, most commonly fish bones. This was a deep deposit and the discovery of several superimposed layers of these vessels suggests some sort of collapse, possibly of shelves in a storeroom."

The overall plan of NSGH appears to be a core domestic unit consisting of a vestibule (2) or foyer, two main rooms (5 and 6), or possibly a main living room (5) and an open-air bakery (6), and possibly a sleeping room (7). Added to the core unit are two magazines (Rooms 2 and 4), and an access corridor (Room 3) that the inhabitants may have also used for storage.

West of the house proper is a space ("Room" 1) about 1.75 m wide and longer than 6 m, extending from the south wall of North Street for an unknown distance to the south beyond the limits of our excavation. This appears to be a street or passageway. NSGH sits as a discrete unit within a larger enclosure formed by the western wall of Gallery Set II (to which NSGH attaches), the southern wall of North Street, and the western wall [3185] of this passage running outside NSGH on the west.

Faience Working Area (Part of EOG)

Remnants of Egypt's oldest known faience workplace happened to escape the teeth of the modern backhoe that gouged the trench (the "backhoe trench"—BHT) in which we were first alerted to the bakeries in 1991. We cleared these remains in 2001 at the bottom of the trench. The older architectural phase that includes the faience-working material extends under the Hypostyle Hall on the west and under the bread mold dumps on the east. In 2002 Angela Milward-Jones excavated a bit of this older phase under the eastern wall of the Hypostyle Hall at the northern side of the BHT (see fig. 1).

This season Milward-Jones and Brian Hunt supervised excavations at the eastern edge of the backhoe trench to expose the older phase of settlement in hopes of learning more about the context of this faience work (Milward-Jones 2004) (Squares 4.F–G-20–22, fig. 1). This meant that we first had to remove the thick stratified layer of dump from the nearby bakeries. We chose a trench about 4 m north-south × 3 m east-west. The layer of sherds was so thick and dense that one day's digging produced 132 sandbags full of pottery.

One of the series of fieldstone pedestals protrudes from the eastern section of the trench. This pedestal is about 40 cm high, 60 cm wide, and 1.30 m long. It is the last of a series of pedestals stretching in a line eastward, the northernmost row in several rows of pedestals across the western side of EOG (see below).

A trampled floor extends from the base of the pedestal. Two little trenches run westward, on line with the sides of the pedestal. These little trenches must be the equivalent of the narrow, shallow trenches that run along the bases of the pedestals in the building we excavated in 1988–'89 in our Area AA (now part of SFW, see fig. 1).

The pedestals in AA still retained a marl clay plaster on the sides. One still had a marl-plastered top. Gray alluvial clay marked where single brick partitions divided the top of the pedestal in quadrants. The marl clay just stopped, or lipped up, where the partition wall had been (Lehner 1992: 22–25). It appears that small bins or compartments stood upon the pedestals, not directly, but straddling the spaces between the pedestals. As with storage platforms from elsewhere in the ancient world, the aim appears to have been to have air circulate below the compartments, while keeping the stored material high and dry. Small stones and sherds filled the little trenches running continuously at floor level along the bases of the pedestals in AA. This may have been to facilitate draining and soaking away of any water than ran down. There were also small circular features, possibly postholes, in the little trench or gutter just in front of the spaces between the pedestals.

Below the trampled floor Milward-Jones found a slightly mounded deposit of pinkish slag-like material. A layer of this same kind of pinkish slag material shows in the section left by the backhoe to the south, hard up against the bakeries. It appears similar to pinkish slag-like material that University of Pennsylvania excavators Steve Harvey and Matthew Adams found in faience-working hearths at Abydos (Nicholson and Peltenburg 2000: 180–81). Is it related to the patches of a faience working area that we salvaged from the backhoe trench lower down? A bit of the same kind of material occurs in the floor where we found the faience material at the bottom of the backhoe trench.

Milward-Jones did not excavate into the pinkish material of the lower phase. So the question of whether this material relates to faience-working nearby must remain for a subsequent season.

East of the Galleries (EOG)

Ashraf Abd el-Aziz supervised excavations along a transect from Gallery Set IV and the 1991 bakeries to the Eastern Town to understand the stratigraphic connections (fig. 1).

His excavations were in the D-tier of grid 4. At the west end is a trench that we excavated in 1991 (then called A7/16) through masses of discarded bread molds (Lehner 1993: 61–63). This trench is against the eastern side of the bakeries that we found in 1991. The fragments of bread molds and other pottery were probably discards from the activity in those bakeries and other bakeries to the north, cut by a separate backhoe trench, known as BBHT2. Abd el-Aziz excavated in alternating squares to the east, linking up in Square 4.D28 with the Eastern Town House excavations of Dan Hounsell and Emma Hancox.

Abd el-Aziz's excavators first removed very compact silty sand from the surface, the result of Nile inundation waters reaching this part of the site, possibly as recently as the early 20th century AD. Repeated saturation with Nile floodwaters compressed, compacted, and homogenized this gray mud with concentrations of fragmented pottery. This cemented "settlement sludge" increases to the northeast across our site.

At the west end of his transect, in Square 4.D22–23, Abd el-Aziz's excavations took in a row of the curious fieldstone pedestals, each about 50 or 60 cm wide and a little more than a meter long (figs. 6, 7). A very thin (35 cm) wall runs parallel and 1.25 m north of the pedestals. In 2002 we mapped rows of pedestals and such parallel

Mark Lehner

Figure 6. East of the galleries (EOG), looking northwest. In the foreground pedestals emerge as workmen scrape the surface.

thin walls in the E- and F-tiers just north of Abd el-Aziz's transect. One of the pedestals belonging to the series that Abd el-Aziz excavated is founded 60 cm deep in the east section of our 1991 trench, A7/16 (now Square 4.D21).

The Pedestals

Abd el-Aziz found a large cache of animal bone in Square 4.D25 in the vicinity of the fieldstone pedestals. In 2004 we recognized that the pattern of the pedestals—two rows separated by a thin wall or line of single fieldstones that runs down the center of the space between the rows—exists over a much wider area across the southern 45 m of EOG. Starting in Abd el-Aziz's east-west C-tier in grid 4 and moving north we see the following sequence:

- thin line of single fieldstones
- clear corridor, 90 cm wide
- row of pedestals, 1.26 m wide
- clear corridor, 1.20 m wide
- thin line of single fieldstones, 35 cm wide
- clear corridor, 1.10 m wide
- row of pedestals, 1.24 m wide
- clear (sherd-filled) corridor, 1.10 m wide

- thin line of single fieldstones, 25 to 35 cm wide
- clear corridor, 1.10 to 1.14 m wide
- row of pedestals, 1.20 m wide
- clear corridor, 90 cm wide
- thin line of fieldstones, 25 to 30 cm wide
- clear corridor, 90 cm wide
- row of pedestals in the excavations for the older phase (see above)

As far as we have cleared in southern EOG we have four rows of the peculiar pedestals, the longest run being 12 pedestals in Squares 4.C23–24. We have yet to scrape and map where our 2002 camp and access roads were located, so there are likely more of the series in southern EOG.

The pedestals are built onto, and into, the thick layer of sherds (70% bread mold fragments according to ceramicist Anna Wodzińska's count from excavated parts). Considering Abd el-Aziz's cache of animal bone, could the pedestals have been for butchering? The cache was notable for numerous teeth and perhaps other non-meat-bearing bone, which we would expect butchers to discard. On the other hand, Abd el-Aziz also found a patch of concentrated pigment in the area, which may

Figure 7. A pedestal seen in profile in the area east of the galleries (EOG), looking east. The new high security wall around the Giza Plateau can be seen in the background. Beyond is the village of Nazlet es-Semman.

Mark Lehner

have been ground on one of the pedestals. The inhabitants might have used the pedestals for a variety of purposes.

Complex History of EOG Dumping

The large rectangular area from Main Street to the Royal Administrative Building (about 75 m north-south) and from the Gallery Complex to the Eastern Town (35 m east-west) was used for industry and for dumping waste. The stratigraphy is complex.

In our trench A7/16 that we excavated immediately east of the bakeries in 1991, we see several phases of crude buildings composed of fieldstone (Lehner 1993: 61, fig. 5). There are one or two pedestals that appear to be founded on an earlier, deeper surface than those in Abd el-Aziz's transect. There are walls built against dumped sherds—mostly bread molds. The southern walls of the bakeries were founded upon layers of discarded sherds, "bread mold gravel," about 13 cm thick. The eastern wall of the eastern bakery was set upon some of the dumped sherd-rich trash and shows a foundation trench cut through some of this trash. The inhabitants built the bakery walls in trenches cut down into an area already laden with discarded pottery from earlier bread-baking.

The combined west and east walls of the two bakeries extend south as the walls of Gallery IV.11, the eastern most gallery in Set IV. These walls, entirely built of fieldstone as opposed to the other gallery walls of mudbrick, were probably added on, a later addition, to an older Gallery Set IV. Meanwhile, the work of Astrid Huser and Ana Tavares in the area of Square 6.W19 (fig. 1) indicates that the thicker western wall of Gallery IV-11 is itself older than the outer fieldstone wall of the Royal Administrative Building.

Connection with the Eastern Town

At the far eastern end of his transect, Abd el-Aziz found a corridor between two mudbrick walls 1.50 m apart. The eastern wall of this corridor runs south where it was picked up by Dan Hounsell and Emma Hancox as the western wall of a court (H) in front of the structure that we call Eastern Town House (fig. 8).

The Eastern Town House (ETH)

In 2002 we barely ascertained the existence of the Eastern Town before the trench for the new high security wall was dug along the modern road on the eastern part of our site. This season our goal was to excavate and to sample material culture intensively to understand the nature of the habitations and how life in the Eastern Town differed from that in the galleries. We wanted evidence about the life span of the town. Did people live on here after the royal house had abandoned the royal building and the galleries

and moved away from Giza at the end of Menkaure's reign?

We chose to excavate one of the house compounds. Dan Hounsell and Emma Hancox supervised excavations in a 10 × 10-m area (Squares 4.B–C29–30) that took in one discrete house complex (figs. 8, 9).

Burials in ETH

A series of burial pits turned up in the far eastern side of the 10 × 10-m area. Jessica Kaiser, Johnny Karlsson, and Tove Björk excavated nine burials. The pits are narrow, sub-rectangular (oval) in plan, rather bell-shaped in section, and generally oriented east-west with the heads to the west. All are closer to one another in orientation than the Late Period (c. 664–332 BC) burials, so numerous in the northwestern part of the site. Only one of these burials had a burial object. Burial 361, a child around three years old, had a coin in the fill about 5 cm above the skull. The coin is too corroded to see the imprint, but it may date these burials, possibly to the Graeco-Roman period. It is also possible the burials are Christian.

The burial pits are cut 90 cm deep into the mud mass. The cuts show about 1 m of Old Kingdom settlement layers over very clean sand (the bottom of the settlement?).

ETH House Layout

The structure we selected for excavation this season turned out to be one discrete compound.

ETH has a core domestic unit that measures 3.60 m east-west × 5.30 m (about 10 cubits) north-south (fig. 8). An entrance opens at about the center of the west side to a small vestibule or foyer (B2). A turn left then right gave access into a main north-south room (B1-G1), about 5.30 × 2.20 m, with a marl-plastered low bench against the eastern wall. The inhabitants built the bench in two stages, first as a bin lined with a thin wall. They extended the bin into the room, then filled it and plastered over the top. It is possible that the bench (a true mastaba like the benches in contemporary village houses) first functioned like the small rectangular bins or fireplaces we have found in gate houses, gallery houses, and the houses along the western side of the Hypostyle Hall. Another right turn at the far southern end of the main room gave access to a niche (G) set off by a low partition wall or banister a single brick thick. Inside the niche a raised platform, about 2.10 × 1.10 m, may have been for sleeping, like the bed platforms found in other houses of the Old, Middle, and New Kingdoms.

In the ETH house, the entrance foyer (B2) is on the northwest and the sleeping niche is on the southwest. Hounsell pointed out that the SFE house plan (see below), as yet only a pattern in the mud mass, shows what might be a similar core domestic unit, but turned 180°

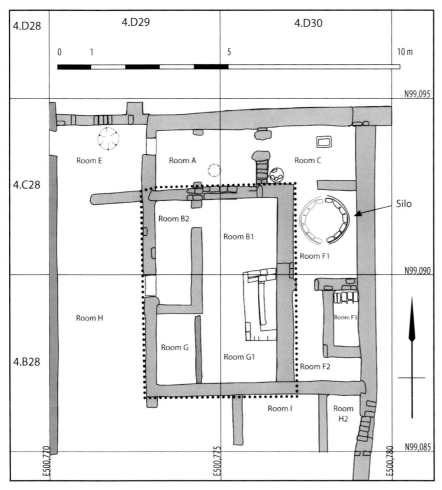

Figure 8. Plan of the Eastern Town House. The core domestic unit is outlined with the dotted line.

so that the entrance foyer is on the southeast and the sleeping niche, if it be that, is on the northeast. The core unit in SFE (foyer, main room, and sleeping niche) is 5.15 m (about 10 cubits) north-south and 3.40 m east-west—just about the same size as the core domestic unit in ETH. The hypothetical sleeping niche in SFE is 1.05 m (2 cubits) × 2.00 m, also similar in size to the one in ETH.

We see this same pattern of foyer, main room, and sleeping niche in the houses tucked into the south ends of Gallery II.2, perhaps in Gallery II.4, and in Gallery III.8 (where the inhabitants carried out small scale copper-work in one of the rear industrial chambers). It is a simple form of the divided-court plan, or "snail house," the rudiments of which are reflected in the alphabetical hieroglyph for "h."

Small courts and chambers for storage and industry surround the core domestic unit of the ETH house. An L-shaped series of five small courts and chambers, three along the north and two along the east side, was entered from the southwest. Each had small installations, such as mud-lined pits, and little platforms. Dark ash filled the central room (A).

Figure 9. The Eastern Town House, looking northwest from the southeastern corner.

The room in the northeast corner (C) had a limestone basin and a small ceramic vat, about 42 cm in diameter, buried to its rim in a floor. A turn to the right (south) put one into a chamber or enclosure (F1), about 2.5 (north-south) × 2 (east-west) m in which the team found the remains of a mud-lined circle composed of single bricks, about 1.10 m in diameter. One of the Late Period or Christian Period graves cut the circle. We think this is most likely the bottom of a grain storage silo, such as the remains of silos—about 2 cubits (1.05 m) in diameter—which we found in other parts of the Eastern Town in 2002. Beyond this chamber to the south another chamber (F2) contains a rectangular bin (F3), 1 × 1.9 m, built into the northeast corner. This may be like the rectangular bins we see in other houses across our site. Could it have been for storage or was it used as an enclosure for grinding grain into flour?

Another L-shaped series of courts and chambers wraps around the west and south sides of the core domestic unit. A doorway on the east gave access to this series through a small foyer (H2) whence you stepped down onto a stone step into an ashy chamber (I). A wing wall partitioned this from another open ashy space to the west, which opened, in turn, to the largest court (H), along the entire west side, some 6 m long and 2.60 (5 cubits) m wide.

The Northwest Corner of the Royal Building, Area 6.W19

Ana Tavares and Astrid Huser continued excavations in the area of the northwestern corner of the Royal Administrative Building (RAB) to link up the stratigraphic relations across the site (fig. 10). The excavation of this square links the stratigraphic relations between our Areas WCE (east of the Wall of the Crow) and WCS (south of the Wall of Crow), by way of the Enclosure Wall around the west and south of the Gallery Complex, with the Royal Administrative Building and Gallery Set IV, the bakeries we found in 1991, the Hypostyle Hall, and beyond.

This team has been exploring the many junctures of walls and floors in this spot with small probe excavations.

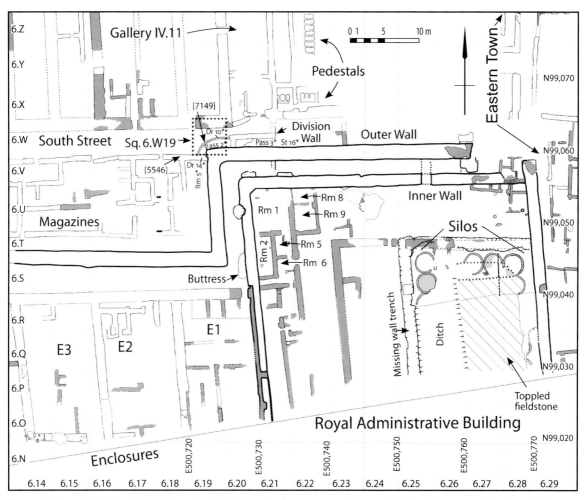

Figure 10. Plan of the Royal Administrative Building and adjacent areas. Feature labels with an asterisk refer to Table 1.

They ascertained that the inner wall of the two parallel RAB fieldstone walls was built on an earlier mudbrick wall. The earlier mudbrick wall bounded a courtyard [20,876] on its west, possibly belonging to a large mudbrick structure (house?) to the east. Some of the early phase structures inside the RAB northwestern corner may belong to this layout before the RAB existed. Post-holes in the courtyard suggest lightweight wood and reed structures.

This mudbrick complex was built and functioned about the same time as Gallery IV.11. At its northern end the western wall of Gallery IV.11 is also the western wall of the bakeries that we excavated in 1991. This completes the stratigraphic link to the excavations in the bakeries and to our investigations throughout the Hypostyle Hall.

The two thick, parallel-running fieldstone walls of the RAB were built and functioned at the same time. Subsequently a thinner fieldstone wall, the Division Wall [546], divided the already narrowed east end of South Street (fig. 10). The Division Wall runs east-west, parallel to the north outer wall of RAB. About the same time they built the Division Wall, the builders made the first fieldstone wall [5546] to the west of the RAB belonging to the South Street Magazines. Later, the curved mudbrick wall [7149] connected the Division Wall and the first wall [5546] of the South Street Magazines to the west. It was this curved wall that first alerted us to the northwest corner of the RAB in Spring 2001.

The bottleneck passage formed by the curved mudbrick wall constricts the eastern end of South Street with the L-shaped southern end of the western wall of the last gallery (IV.11) to the east in Gallery Set IV.

In their final building stage, the inhabitants built a fieldstone structure to the north of the RAB that includes more of the small fieldstone pedestals such as occur in rows and series farther north in EOG (see above).

Ten major phases result from the study of the stratigraphy in the area of 6.w19, as shown in Table 1.

The Royal Administrative Building, Interior Northwest Corner

Freya Sadarangani, James Taylor, and Hala Said supervised excavations in the northwest corner of the

Figure 11. Freya Sadarangani, upper right, James Taylor, and Astrid Huser, front and center, in the early stages of the 2004 RAB excavation. Huser maps a probe, expanded from an intrusive pit, outside the west inner wall of the RAB. The wall next to Huser was originally a mudbrick wall and was later capped with fieldstones. Looking east into the RAB partially backfilled.

Mark Lehner

Table 1. Ten Major Stratigraphic Phases in the Area of Square 6.W19

Phase I: Pre-Building
Natural sand deposits (accumulation of aeolian and waterborne [?] sand, nearly sterile at a fairly high level that might reflect the natural topography of the site)
Phase II: Building Gallery IV.11 and Domestic Space to South
IIa
Building Gallery IV.11 and mudbrick layout to the south (early phase of mudbrick walls in northwestern corner of RAB and courtyard)
IIb
Occupation south of Gallery IV.11 in courtyard to the west of the complex in the early architectural phase of RAB, northwestern corner
IIc
Rebuilding of denuded (or cut down?) mudbrick western wall of RAB
Phase III: Abandonment
Brief period of abandonment evidenced by aeolian sand in all the sondages and in the interface of the three different building phases of the west wall of RAB
Phase IV: Fieldstone Rebuilding
IVa
Masonry rebuilding of the RAB:
Rebuilding inner wall in fieldstone
Building the Enclosure Wall (to effect double fieldstone walls around northwest corner) and masonry repair of Gallery IV
IVb
Occupation of the street between RAB (west wall) and Enclosure Wall
Phase V: South Street Magazines
Va
Construction of South Street Magazines room to the east of RAB enclosure wall and constriction of South Street with the construction of the partition walls
Vb
Intensive occupation of Rm 5* and Passages 2* and 3* (fine fish bone deposits, sequence of fine floors)
Phase VI: Remodeling
VIa
Remodeling Rm 5* and Passages 2* and 3*. Thick sherd deposit raises the level throughout the area. General leveling of Street 16*
VIb
Occupation with Rm 5* used for storage and Passage 2* still functioning with Doorways 10* and 14.* The character of occupation is "shoddy." Outside surface renewed to function with "guard house" and possibly with structures to the north
Phase VII: Curved Mudbrick Wall
VIIa
Leveling the street and new street surface
VIIb
Building the masonry curved retaining wall (implying the decommissioning of structures to the east of Gallery IV.11)
Phase VIII: Pedestal Building and Leveling
VIIIa
Extensive leveling with sherd deposits in Squares 6.X21, 22, and 23 (or accumulation of sherd deposits, infill of structures to the north of south street and east of Gallery Set IV)
VIIIb
Stone capping, representing an extensive construction phase that differs markedly from the preceding masonry structures. Pedestal building and industrial area—extensive, up to EOG in the north
Phase IX: Dismantling
Dismantling of the pedestal building, reuse of all well-cut blocks, occasional ones still *in situ*. Concurrent dismantling of RAB upper levels including masonry, mudbrick, and timber elements
Phase X: Denudation of Site
Denuding, leveling of the site (by the British Army and subsequent sand-quarrying activity? Post-holes, animal tracks, etc.)

* See figure 10 for the location of these features.

Royal Administrative Building (RAB) (figs. 10, 11). They found more evidence of royal administration, including the better part of an actual cylinder seal of dark hard ceramic material incised with a design. The workers found the cylinder seal in a sherd-rich, ashy deposit in the northwestern court (Room 1). Sealings from the broken up floor of Room 9 included one with Khafre's Horus name. More clay sealings came from the excavations in all the rooms and courts. The sealings continue to offer evidence of administrative activities in the RAB enclosure.

Three Rectangular Units of Later Phase

The RAB is not so much a single structure as a great enclosure that must have contained accommodations for those who worked inside.

While it is certainly possible that the function of the courts and chambers changed from more administrative to more domestic over time, rooms in the northwestern corner might have formed three discrete roofed units in the later phases of the area.

Room 2

One of these units is the chamber provisionally designated Room 2, against the western, inner RAB fieldstone wall (fig. 10). The low remains of a wall divide Room 2 into a front and back half, but this low wall may belong to an earlier structure that existed before Room 2 was created. In phase with Room 2 in the south half, is a rectangular feature (50 cm × 1 m) molded in the floor with a low shoulder, partially lined with marl that contains two small, slightly oval depressions. In 2002 we found a small red ware ceramic vat, 42 cm in diameter, sunk into the floor, and this may be part of the installation, attached at its southeastern corner. The northern half of Room 2 contains a deep conical socket or depression, lined with mud, perhaps where a ceramic vessel was removed. Two small ceramic jars remain *in situ* against the dividing wall of Room 2. If this dividing wall is in phase with Room 2, it gives a front and rear part to an oblong unit, similar to houses known from other sites and periods in Egyptian archaeology. Room 2 measures 2.26 × 2.62 m, about 4 × 5 cubits.

Rooms 5–6

Rooms 5 and 6 may form another rectangular domicile, about 6.80 m north-south × 2.20 m east-west. A wall, as thick as the exterior walls of the unit, separates Room 5 from 6, with an entrance toward the east side. In 2002 we found a curious semi-circular feature attached to the north wall of Room 5, just beside a doorway that opens into the northwestern court (Room 1). Sadarangani and Taylor removed this and excavated down to an older floor level.

Room 5

In an earlier phase than that of the semi-circular feature, the excavators found two rectangular installations, a matching pair, situated just inside the doorway that opens into Room 5 from Room 1. These might have been used as hearths or fireplaces, or, they might be negative patterns from features that were removed. The team found no ash in the one to the west, but discovered two layers, one very rich in pottery sherds, in the one to the east, which measures 1.45 north-south × 0.70 m east-west. Remains of mudbricks lined the south side of the eastern installation. These two rectangular features may belong to a class of low rectangular, brick-lined bins or installations that we have found in houses all across the site. A mud-lined circular hole, 43 cm in diameter, in the middle of Room 5 may have been an emplacement for a small vat like that in Room 6 and in Room C in the Eastern Town House.

Room 6

In Room 6, to the south of Room 5, the excavators found in the northwest corner a rectangular hearth, 1 × 1.10 m, with a dark, ashy fill (Phase 05: Occupation A). Small stones lined the hearth against the north and west walls of the room. A single course of mudbricks lined the east side (the end bricks were removed).

In a later period the inhabitants partitioned Room 6 (Phase 6) by constructing a dog-legged, two-course, mudbrick wall [4057] east to west making the southern end of the room into a kind of platform. They also bordered an eastern mudbrick hearth [2954]. A circular depression in the east side of the platform might have been for a small vat. It is 42 cm in diameter, just the diameter of a vat sunken into the floor of Room C in the Eastern Town House, and, closer at hand, a vat in the lower floor (off the bench) at the west side of Room 6.

Rooms 8–9

The combination of Rooms 8 and 9 may be yet a third roofed unit, about 6 m north-south × 2.30 m east-west. A single doorway gives access to this unit, opening in the eastern wall of Room 8 from the open area to the east, the area north of the sunken court of silos in the RAB. (A doorway shown in the eastern wall of Room 9 on the Season 2002 map proved to be a mistake). A small vat is embedded in the southeastern corner of Room 9.

Units 2, 5–6, 8–9 as Domiciles?

Room 2 opens onto the court (Room 1) in the northwestern corner of the RAB. The Room 5–6 unit opens onto the same court and also to the open court on the east, stretched lengthwise north-south. The unit comprised of Rooms 8–9 opens to the court located east and north of the sunken court of silos. The courts provided open space and light for various kinds of work.

We hypothesized that Rooms 2, 5–6, and 8–9 might comprise three bipartite domestic units, each with a front and back (though the wall that divides Room 2 may not be of the same period as the other walls of this structure).

The Eastern Court: Rows of Holes

In the court east of the unit comprised of Rooms 5 and 6 and west of the sunken silo court, at the southern limit of the excavations, Sadarangani cleared a series of small holes in rows forming a grid patch oriented, charmingly, like all the great architectural layouts at our site, slightly west of north. The holes are 9 to 11 cm in diameter at the top, conical in section, comprising a patch about 1.25 × 2 m, seven holes to an east-west row. The grid of holes looks like the rows of little sockets for a pebble game, such as are found in ancient buildings. These holes in a mud court are most likely sockets for small ceramic vessels. In fact the holes are similar to others around a molded shallow circular depression in the top of the mud platform at the southern end of Room 6. The bottoms of conical jars remain in the holes on the platform.

Magazines of the Earlier Phases

Room 1 is the open area or court just inside the northwestern corner of the RAB (fig. 10). Three ephemeral floors mostly showed in the southeastern corner of Room 1. By the end of February, Sadarangani and Taylor found under these floors a series of three magazines or storage chambers. The magazines line up along the western side of Room 1, leaving an open space or court (Room F) on the east 2.60 m (5 cubits) wide east-west, and more than 5.94 m long north-south just north of Rooms 5–6 (the northern limits lie under the northern fieldstone RAB wall).* Various artifacts turned up scattered across the floors of these small magazines.

Room A, the magazine in the far northwest corner measures 1.26 north-south × 1.80 m east-west. The doorway on the east is 52 cm (1 cubit) wide. Artifacts on the floor included a spouted vessel, red pigment, fallen red-painted wall plaster, sandstone pieces (perhaps abraders), the broken end of a small (8 cm wide) saddle quern, and, from the tumble layer above the floor, yellow ochre.

Room B, the middle magazine measures 1.14 m east-west × 2.12 m north-south. The doorway on the north end of the east side is 52 cm wide with a limestone pivot socket on the inner north side. Another doorway at the southwest corner (partially under the later west fieldstone

wall of the RAB) was also 52 cm wide. Parts of flat, round bread-baking trays lay in the tumble fill just above the floor level.

Room C, the southern magazine, is 2.14 m north-south × 1.40 m east-west. The doorway on the north end of the east side, opening to Room F, is 58 cm wide with a limestone pivot socket on the inner north side. A doorway on the northwest to Room D is 52 cm wide. The following objects lay on the floor: a straight-rim jar, three cylindrical jar stands, a stone hammer, lumps of basalt and flint (one each), and a pillow stone. The small rectangular pillow stones with rounded corners form a class of artifact with examples from across the site. However, we do not know their function.

Being of an earlier phase than the main inner fieldstone wall of the RAB, the magazines backed to an earlier marl-plastered mudbrick wall which runs lower and parallel to the main fieldstone wall, leaving a space 32 to 53 cm wide and about 2 m long. It is possible that the magazines end on the west, at the mudbrick wall capped by the core of the inner west fieldstone wall of the RAB.

A marl-lined doorway opens in the mudbrick wall on the west side of the magazines, Rooms A-B-C. This doorway opened from the middle magazine to the west. This entrance did not function when the large inner fieldstone wall of the royal building was constructed. When the inhabitants made the doorway, and probably when they built all three magazines, there was no large fieldstone wall of the royal building. The thick, double, fieldstone enclosure walls of the royal building are later, thrown up around and over a mudbrick complex that already existed.

RAB Phasing: Administrative to Domestic?

The series of magazines stretching north in the earlier phases of the walls underlying the floors of Room 1 were part of a broader complex that comprised more than Rooms A through I. This complex must have functioned together with the alluvial mud court that Ana Tavares and Astrid Huser found west of the inner fieldstone wall, but of an architectural phase that predates the RAB wall.

It is possible that a layout given over to administration and storage was later converted to more domestic use, and this might be reflected in the plant and animal remains from this excavation. The irony—or confusion in our understanding—is that Rooms 2, 5–6, and 8–9 might look more house-like just when the inhabitants erected the thick double enclosure walls around this complex and around the sunken court of silos farther east.

---

* A plan of the earlier phase based on the 2005 excavations is shown in the preliminary report on the 2005 field season (Lehner, Kamel, and Tavares 2006: 56).

3. Clearing and Excavation of New Areas Around the Soccer Field

Our large-scale clearing in this 2004 season focused on two major areas: west of the soccer field, where we discovered a large previously unknown section of the ancient city, and north of the Wall of the Crow. We now have a total of 1,635 5 × 5-m squares staked out. We staked about 400 squares this season. The total staked area is thus about 4 hectares. We have not established the grid over the larger area of the whole site.

Our clearing of the overburden with front loaders and trucks nearly surrounded the Abu Hol Sports Club (or soccer field). We began on the east, just inside the gate of the new (as of 2002) high security wall. We could not clear southward along the east side of the soccer field because the road giving access to our site, and to Dr. Zahi Hawass's site of the Workers' Cemetery, runs here before curving around south of the club to head north along the west edge of the site (fig. 12). This route was necessary after we took up the paved road along the north side of the soccer field. We cleared west along the north side of the soccer field. We next turned south along the west of the soccer field. We cleared a very broad swath, 60 m east-west and nearly 200 m north-south (although this cleared area is not a perfect rectangle).

Altogether this season we cleared, staked, and mapped 1.2 hectare east, north, and west of the soccer field. The newly discovered Western Town (Area SFW, west of the

Yukinori Kawae

Figure 12. Clearing overburden from around the southwestern end of the Abu Hol Sports Club soccer field, which is behind the line of tamarisk trees on the left. The new access road to our site and the Workers' Cemetery can be seen on the right. The high security wall holds the town back from the archaeological zone of the low desert. View to the southeast.

contractor Farahat's smaller loader and two trucks clearing the massive pile of modern refuse south of the soccer field. Thanks to an incentive system that Field Director Mohsen Kamel started, the crews worked fast and furiously. Mohammed Musilhi's team worked from the east. Farahat's crew continued from the west. As the loaders bit into the mound, great clouds of fine dust and ash filled the air. Farahat's section through the modern dump increased in height from 5.6 m (end of March) to 7 m (May), consisting entirely of modern stable dumping and garbage of various sorts. Eventually the two truck and loader crews met, having eliminated the modern dump for a span of some 40 m south of the south retaining wall of the soccer field, which we left free-standing, retaining nothing. More of the dump remains to be cleared farther south sloping down to the access road that curves around the base of the dump.

South of the soccer field the loaders cleared just down to the clean sand layer that covers the ruins of the ancient city. We left the clean sand as a protective blanket until our return.

In the following sections we describe the features of the ancient settlement as we see them in the "mud mass," or surface of the ruins, without excavation, except for limited excavations west of the soccer field (SFW) and north of the Gate in the Wall of the Crow (WCGN).

Yukinori Kawae

Figure 13. The towering pile of overburden at the south end of the soccer field, which is visible in the background on the right. Our clearing cut a 7-m high section through dumps of the last few decades. View to the northwest.

soccer field) takes in about a hectare by itself. We know that the ancient settlement extends under the soccer field, which covers another 1.2 hectares, so we have ascertained another 2.4 hectares belonging to the total known ancient settlement, now about 7.6 hectares in area.

Around the southwestern corner of the soccer field, the clearing encountered a very high, linear berm of stable dumping and trash that extended the length of the south side of the club (fig. 13). The members of the club built a stone and cement retaining wall to hold back the trash. The people of the stables had been allowed to dump here over a long period, as a strategy, Lehner was told, to prevent the expansion of the sports club farther south.

After Mohammed Musilhi finished clearing the sandy overburden north of the Gate in the Wall of the Crow, his big red loader and the three trucks joined private

East of the Soccer Field (SFE)

Mohammed Musilhi removed the protective piles of sand where the old gate from the modern street was located at the southeastern corner of the site. We took up the asphalt of the modern road along the front of the sports club, now enclosed by the security wall with a gate, both new as of 2002. We cleared the sand and the overburden down to the ancient surface as far as the north side of the new gate. This allowed us to map more of the southern end of the Eastern Town.

Once the heavy machinery removed the asphalt road around the northeast corner of the soccer club, Mohsen had *Reis* ("Overseer") Ahmed and his men clear the sandy overburden down to the mud mass in a corridor 15.60 m wide between the 2002 high security wall and the eastern wall of the soccer club. With our sandbags against those walls, we had ancient surface exposed 11 m wide. The clearing runs 20 m south from the northeast corner of the

Mark Lehner

Figure 14. A house plan revealing itself in the mud mass east of the soccer field (SFE) after the surface was cleared and scraped. The soccer field can be seen on the left. View to the north-northwest.

club and ends about 10.50 m north of the gate through the high security wall. As we already knew in 2002 when we mapped ancient walls in the bottom of the trench for the security wall, the ancient settlement remains slope down toward the south.

As Reis Ahmed's men peeled back the last of the sand cover on Wednesday, February 25, the outlines of a 4,500 year-old house revealed itself like a gift, embedded in the slope of the ancient surface (fig. 14). The mudbrick walls stood out light gray, and the fieldstone walls off-white, in the dark, ashy mud, filled with fragments of ancient pottery. The layout of rectangular courts and chambers measures about 7 m east-west by 15 m north-south (fig. 15). The orientation is markedly west of north, more so than the Gallery Complex.

The SFE house plan, as yet only a pattern in the mud mass, shows what might be a core domestic unit with the entrance foyer on the southeast and a small compartment that could be a sleeping niche on the northeast. The core unit (foyer, main room, and sleeping niche) is 5.15 m (about 10 cubits) north-south and 3.40 m east-west—just about the same size as the core domestic unit in ETH. The hypothetical sleeping niche in SFE is 1.05 m (2 cubits) × 2.00 m. Large courts or rectilinear open spaces surround the hypothetical core domestic unit.

The house layout so nicely revealed in SFE belongs to the southerly extension of the Eastern Town, as we called the agglomeration of housing that we found in 2002 along the southeastern part of our site.

North of the Soccer Field (SFN)

The strip where we removed the modern road to the Workers' Cemetery along the northern wall of the Abu Hol Sports Club widens from about 10 m north-south on the east to about 20 m wide at the western end of the club. Cleared of the overburden, the strip, called Soccer Field North (SFN), gives us a profile east to west across the Eastern Town, the Royal Administration Building, into a new area lying north of the Western Town and south of the Enclosure Wall of the Gallery Complex.

More of the Eastern Town
Removing the modern road into the site gave us 10 m more, north-south, and 18.50 m east-west, of the Eastern Town (fig. 15). We gained about 30 × 5 m more of the town to the north, close to the new high security wall, than we could get in 2002. At that time we had to leave a bank of overburden, 1 to 1.70 m thick, up against that wall.

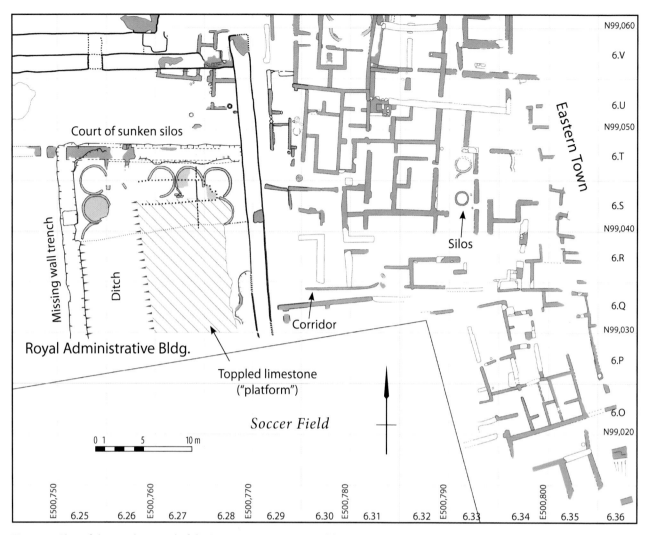

Figure 15. Plan of the southern end of the Eastern Town, Soccer Field East (SFE), showing areas cleared this season, and the east end of the Royal Administrative Building.

The surface of the ancient ruins, or mud mass, near the northeastern corner of the soccer field is 1.75 m lower than the base of the soccer field wall. To insure that the soccer field wall will not collapse in an untimely manner, we have stacked sandbags along the base of the section or cut through the soil, mostly sand, on which the soccer field wall is founded.

Small Domestic Silos
Just as in 2002, when we first peeled off the overburden from the area of the Eastern Town, walls show everywhere. The walls form courts and chambers. In Squares 6.S–T33, two round silos, 1.40 and 1.60 m in diameter, visible in silty soil, appear to fill a courtyard (fig. 15). Right beside the silo on the northeast is a quern or grinding stone of sandstone or quartzite, probably for grinding grain and, to the south, one of the ubiquitous "pillow stones," small rectangular blocks (11 × 16 × 9 cm) with rounded edges and corners. This one might actually be a crude headrest, a version of those so well known

from ancient Egypt. One side is concave for resting the head.

Corridor or Path
A corridor or pathway runs just north of the east end of the northern wall of the soccer field, starting in Square 6.Q29 on the west and running east-west for 30 m. This little lane narrows from 1.30 m wide at the west end to 82 cm wide near the northeast corner of the soccer field. Its northern wall is 30 cm wide, a row of single headers (bricks laid with their short ends to the face of the wall). This wall curves north at the east end, then another short segment, 80 cm long, curves out to the southeast, the two curves making a rounded "v"-shape. A crude, oval limestone basin, 36 × 52 cm, lies embedded in the mud mass 45 cm northeast of the v. The thin north wall swings ever so slightly north on its run to the west, which widens the corridor. The south wall of the corridor is 45 cm thick, a row of stretchers on the north edge and headers on the south edge. This wall ends on the west about 90 cm from

the east wall of the Royal Administration Building (RAB). Here the corridor probably meets another corridor that Paul Sharman and Stephanie Durning mapped farther north in 2002 running north along the east wall of the RAB. But we have yet to scrape and clean this part of the mud mass farther south, so the north-south corridor does not yet show.

(We left most of the Eastern Town that we found in 2002 under a protective blanket of "backfill" sand and a tall conical pile of clean sand for backfilling at the end of this season).

More of the Royal Administrative Building (RAB)

The removal of the road and overburden gave us nearly 15 m more of the RAB ruins north-south to add to the 25 m of RAB that we had north-south in 2002 (fig. 10).

In our strip of newly gained ancient surface, the east wall of RAB, 1.55 m thick, runs strong to the south where it disappears under the Abu Hol Sports Club. Inside the RAB, extends a north-south strip of mud mass, 2.20 to 2.30 m wide. Within this band in the 2002 excavations to the north we found the backs of the eastern row of large round silos, spaced 1.46 m from the RAB east wall (fig. 15). Perhaps a wall, like the one that once ran north and west of the sunken court of silos, once ran along the silos on the east. We have hypothesized that it was a parapet wall, where the inhabitants could walk along the tops of the silos for filling them from the top. At some later point, someone robbed the wall, leaving its very regular foundation trench as a track of its course. We did not find the wall on the east side of the silos in 2002, but here we did not finish the excavation, and we might yet extract the hypothetical parapet on the east of the silos.

At the south end of the newly claimed strip, a little of the backs of two more silos show in the mud mass.

Toppled Stone Wall

Moving west inside the RAB enclosure, we have more of the field of fallen stone, irregular broken stones that the ancient inhabitants used for making fieldstone walls (fig. 15). In 2002 this flat, stony patch looked so consistent, we thought early in our excavations it might be a platform. But Fiona Baker found in her excavation that the "platform" consisted of stones that had toppled off that wall on the north and west sides of the silos court; that is, the hypothetical parapet wall. This stone wall was a rebuilding of an earlier mudbrick wall. It appeared in 2002 that someone had trenched through the silos, purposefully decommissioning them. Then they pushed the fieldstone wall that surrounded them over into the court and on top of the silos. We found the northern silos covered by the stony fill, which was mostly limestone, but included an extraordinary amount of granite.

Since the stony platform falls away to the "Ditch" (see below) on the west, we might think it results from a fieldstone wall that was pushed over from the east, perhaps from that hypothetical eastern parapet wall, or, from the east wall of the RAB itself. Why this toppling left that strip of mud along the east wall of RAB with the backs of the eastern silos and no toppled fieldstone, we do not quite understand. Our new patch of "platform" is 7.50 to 9 m east-west, 10.30 m north-south. The stony layer is 1.30 m thick in the section of our 2002 excavations.

Ditch

On the west side of the sunken silo court, the "platform" of toppled stones is missing, and the ruins of the sunken court look like a shallow ditch, or a U-shaped depression, the east side of which is the irregular edge of the "platform" (figs. 10, 16). The ditch is about 7.50 m wide from the west edge of the "platform" to the east edge of the trench that marks the missing fieldstone wall.

This year, the bottom of the ditch is damp, as are all low areas of the site because the water table seems to have risen since 2002. The muddy sand slopes from the "platform" down 50 to 60 cm to a trough, then up again to the rather straight edge where the parapet wall around the silos was robbed out. We have yet to scrape or clean thoroughly, but no silos show in the mud mass. Baker exposed the silos after excavating much of the 2002 season through the fieldstone "platform" and the mud mass.

Some fieldstones remain in the trench, 1.60 m wide, left from the robbing of the west wall around the silo court. Some fallen stone lies along the west edge of the trench, but not much, a spread about 1.80 m wide and 20 cm thick. The fact that most of the stone from the missing wall is in the "platform" over on the east side of the silos court must indicate that most of the wall material was reused elsewhere, while a segment that stood on the east remained and was the last to topple over.

The alternative is that the "platform" of broken stone once filled the whole area inside the silo court, including what we are calling the "Ditch." Someone removed the material on the west, leaving the "Ditch," in order to use the stone elsewhere. This explanation becomes much more compelling now that we have found evidence of systematic stripping and trenching walls for stone farther west, in Enclosure E5 and the Western Town (see below). Similarly, we found evidence in the Gallery Complex of people systematically stripping mudbricks from walls. The tombs in the Workers' Cemetery up the slope are most obvious possibilities for reuse of the stone and mudbrick.

Western Court

Next, to the west beyond the silos court, still within the RAB, the silty sand surface dips again for a width of about

5 m between the patchy stone tumble from the missing west wall of the silos court to a north-south mudbrick wall showing in the mud mass. This wall, a little over 1 m thick, is a continuation of one that Bob Will and Susan Bain excavated in 2002 in Squares 6.S23 and 6.T23, where it turns 90° and runs east, leaving a doorway at the northwest corner of the silos court (fig. 10). In the newly cleared area to the south (Squares 6.Q–R24) the dip between the walls is a depression about 5 m in diameter.

Administrative Rooms

We continue west, to an area immediately south of the area of intensive excavations this season by Freya Sadarangani, James Taylor, and Hala Said (see above). From where they excavated Rooms 1, 2, 5–6, and 8–9 the surface of the remains slopes southward down under the soccer field. The mudbrick walls that define chambers and courts continue 14.70 m south of the 2002 excavation limit, which is the width here of the strip we gained from the removal of the modern road.

Next we come to the west wall of the RAB. The outer wall of the thick, double fieldstone walls leaves the west side of RAB to head west as the Enclosure Wall at 16.20

m south of the northwest corner of the RAB. We are now farther south in our newly gained strip. Here the inner west wall of the RAB continues as a thinner fieldstone wall, 1 m wide, with a mudbrick accretion on the west, 60 cm wide (figs. 10, 16). Marl plaster covers the west face of the mudbrick accretion. This 1.60 m-thick composite wall shows clearly all the way to our sandbagged section, about 1.60 m tall, through the sand supporting the modern wall around the soccer field. Patches of tumble lie along the east side of the ancient hybrid wall, but a big spread of tumble to the west, 3.4 m wide, indicates that most of the material from the wall toppled to that side.

The Enclosures

Moving to the west, we leave the Royal Administrative Building and enter the first of a series of large rectangular courts or enclosures, defined by thick fieldstone walls running southward under the sports club, so that we do not know the full length of them (figs. 10, 16). Except for the northeast corner of E1 that we revealed in 2002, these enclosures only came to light after our clearing this season.

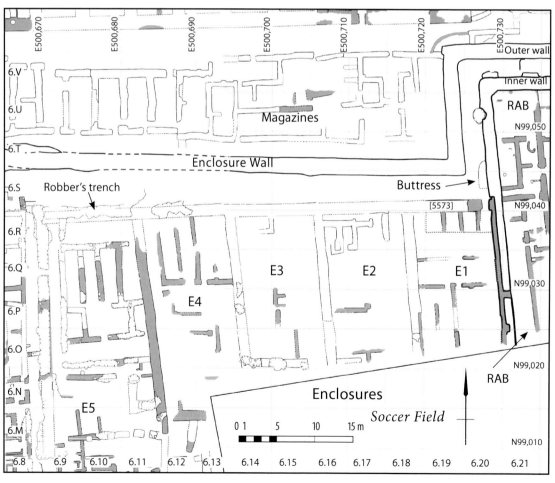

Figure 16. Plan of the Enclosures and adjacent areas.

E1

The west wall of the RAB defines the first enclosure (E1) on the east (figs. 10, 16). Another fieldstone wall that is 1.46 m wide bounds E1 on the west. E1 is 10.20 m wide. The north wall [5573] of E1 is composed of fieldstone and mud and runs east-west parallel to the Enclosure Wall, leaving a corridor 3 m wide. A doorway at the east end of this corridor opens into the northeast corner of E1. Emerging through this doorway from E1, one was confronted by a buttress (fig. 16, the only buttress on the structure formerly called the Buttress Building, now RAB), forcing a turn left, then a turn right into the north-south corridor between the outer and inner western fieldstone walls of the RAB. Thin mudbrick walls, excavated in 2002 in Squares 6.R19–20, run off the northern wall of E1, into the unexcavated enclosure. The "mud mass" fill of E1 is very sandy silt. E1 stretches about 16.30 m from the north wall of the enclosure to the sandbagged section under the northern wall of the soccer field.

When our workers scraped the surface with trowels and cleaned with brushes, they revealed traces of mudbrick walls that subdivide this and the other great enclosures (E2–5) (fig. 17). In E1, mudbrick walls, about 50 cm thick, appeared about 7 to 9 m south of the northern wall. The mudbrick walls seem to form chambers or courts, similar to the situation in the northwest corner of the Royal Administrative Building (RAB). In fact, these enclosures might be part of the same complex; that is, part of the RAB, which would make the royal building even larger than the 50-m width that we saw in 2002.

E2

Next, to the west, is enclosure E2, 10.20 m wide, defined by the fieldstone wall separating it from E1 on the east, and another fieldstone wall, 1.20 to 1.30 m wide, on the west. In the northwest part of E2 a depression in the mud mass is about 5 to 6 m in diameter (wider east-west than north-south). The surface of the mud mass slopes generally down to the middle from the sidewalls—as it does in all the enclosures of this series. The northern wall is a continuation of the north wall of E1. It is hard to see this wall, as it is lost in a sandy depression across the west half of E2. The length from the northern wall to the sandbags below the sports club wall is 18.10 m.

After we scraped and cleaned the surface, we saw thinner fieldstone walls that form a court or chamber, 2.2 × 3 m, in the northwest corner of E2. The chamber hangs off an east-west fieldstone wall that runs parallel to the north wall of E1 and E2, leaving a corridor, 1.60 m wide.

Figure 17. Workmen scrape and brush the surface to expose the walls of Enclosure E5. View to the south.

Mark Lehner

E3

Next, to the west, is E3, the third enclosure, which is 10.20 m wide. E3's east wall is the west wall of E2. We lose this wall under sand about 14 m south of the north wall of E1, E2, and E3. The surface of the mud mass slopes into a trough between the sidewalls of E3. There are two prominent depressions in the mud mass north of a rounded higher shoulder that is about 8.80 to 11.20 m south of the north wall. The northern depression is more prominent. It is oval shaped and oriented east-west. The south depression is less defined, more round, about 7 m in diameter. The west wall of E3 is delineated for a stretch of only 5 to 6 m south of the north wall of E3, but certainly continues as a stony ridge, with a slump of stony tumble to the west about 2 m wide. Material from the decay of the wall rests on clean sand half a meter thick. The sand accumulated against the base of the wall before the material slumped onto it. E3 stretches 20.30 m south to the sandbags against the section, 1.50 above the mud mass, under the soccer field wall. At the southern end of the stretch, there is an east-west fieldstone wall that is 95 cm thick, making E3 18.10 m long north to south.

After we cleaned the ancient surface, and after it dried, we could see internal mudbrick walls that subdivide E3. There seems to be some kind of fieldstone structure in the southwest corner of E3.

E4

Next, to the west, E4 is delimited on the west by a wall that is 1.30 m wide and that appears to be mostly mudbrick. E4 is about 10.70 m wide east-west. The south fieldstone wall of E3 does not continue west across E4. It is not yet clear if the west wall of E4 goes all the way to the common north wall of enclosures E1-2-3. That north wall is not very clear here. It shows as a ragged, rocky ridge on line with the north wall of E1–2. We pick up the west wall of E4 certainly 7.5 m south of the ridge marking the north wall. At 14.80 m to the south, the west wall becomes stonier. At 16 m south, the wall stands high, about 1.50 m above the bottom of the depression at the south end of E4. Mudbrick slumped to both sides of the wall, creating a prominent hard ridge that stood tall in the clean sand as the workmen cleared it. This wall runs south of the north wall for a total of 24.70 m where it turns a corner to jog 4 m west. Then the wall may turn south. We are not certain, but if it does continue south it slopes down to the lower ruins of the Western Town (SFW), lining up with a fieldstone wall, 1.10 m thick, that continues south through Squares 6.G11 to 6.J11 as the east wall of the large house called Unit 3 (see below).

It was in E4 that internal walls of mudbrick showed best after we scraped and cleaned the surface. E4 contains rectangular chambers (fig. 16). A chamber in the northwest corner is 6.40 m north-south × 1.80 m east-west between walls that are 50 and 60 cm thick. The west wall of this chamber forms a corridor, 1.50 m wide, with the west wall of E4. Another chamber is located at the east side of E4. Thinner walls, of which only traces show, subdivide the east chamber. Between the west and east chambers runs a corridor about 1.75 m wide. A mudbrick, marl-lined wall that stretches out 7.3 m perpendicular to the west wall of E4 at the south end may mark a southern boundary of this enclosure.

E5: Magazine Complex in SFNW

West of the west wall of E4, walls form a rectangular complex that contains four long magazines running north-south with additional narrow courts and corridors. At some point someone removed some of the walls down to the foundations, leaving the robbers' trenches as traces of where the walls were located. The whole E5 complex is 11.50 m wide (east-west) on the north, 13.30 m wide on the south, and 17.60 m long (north-south).

An east-west fieldstone wall runs parallel to the outer Enclosure Wall, which is the north wall of the Enclosures (E1–4), leaving a court 2.40 m wide (north-south) × 11.50 m long (east-west). The four magazines lie to the south of this court. Each magazine is about 1.50 m wide (east-west) × 7.20 m north-south. On the west, a band of mud, 1.30 m wide, certainly looks like a wall. But this band is actually the "mud mass" that accumulated on the floor of the north-south corridor or fifth magazine. When someone robbed out the fieldstone walls on either side, they left the raised mud looking like a wall itself. The fieldstone wall on the west, which was the west wall of the magazine complex, is marked by the robber's trench, 1.30 to 1.40 m wide. The robber removed almost all of the stones of the wall. This trench continues southward 15 m into the area of SFW (Soccer Field West) where we mapped the remains of the Western Town (see below).

E5 marks the interface between the Enclosures west of the Royal Administrative Building and the Western Town.

The Enclosures: Magazines or Elite Gallery Houses?

One hypothesis about the function of the enclosures is that they contain magazines for storage. Another is that they are iterations of the situation excavated this season by Freya Sadarangani and James Taylor in the northwest corner of the RAB—courts, chambers, and magazines for working and living, production, and administration. A third hypothesis is that the Enclosures are larger, more elite versions of the galleries to the north. Houses are tucked into the back, southern, ends of the galleries, and, behind the houses are chambers for cooking, roasting, and baking. The Enclosures may be larger, more upscale versions of the galleries, with larger houses and production facilities in the southern parts.

If the Enclosures are iterations of the assemblages of courts and chambers such as we excavated in the northwest corner of the RAB, we have just increased nearly tenfold the area of such facilities, with all their complex phasing (see above). Consider that the facilities in the northwest corner of the RAB themselves continue at least another 10 or 15 m farther south, and they lie in an enclosure, just over 10 m wide, between the silo court and the inner west wall of the RAB. Enclosures 1 through 4, each just over 10 m wide, comprise four more zones, nearly 10 × 20 m, each of which may have contained the same kinds of activities and similar complex phasing. All of this could be one large complex, part of the royal enclosure that we call RAB.

Another possibility is that these enclosures were similar in function to the enclosures in the northern part of the Western Extension, north of Main Street, west of Gallery Sets I and II, and south of the Wall of the Crow, in what we called the Eastern Compound (see fig. 1). The fieldstone walls that define the northern enclosures are not as well preserved, but there were four in the north, and like the southern Enclosures, each was slightly more than 10 m (20 cubits) wide.

West of the Soccer Field (SFW): The Western Town

In our 2003 study and report-writing season, we limited our excavations to two trenches through the sandy overburden right up against the west side of the soccer field (Lehner 2003). We stopped at the compact "mud mass" where we could see ancient mudbrick and fieldstone walls of what appeared to be large houses.

During the 2004 season we cleared the thick overburden along the west side of the soccer field. Much of this overburden is waste dumped from the nearby riding stables in the late 1990s. This sloped down to the west where the overburden was almost nonexistent, and modern paper and gravel for a roadbed came to lie almost directly over the ruins of the ancient town. Where the sand diggers from the stables left the surface nearly exposed, walls and floors of the ancient settlement were within centimeters of the surface, and in some parts the surface was the dust of the disintegration of the ruins. Our workers cleared by hand the scant sandy cover from the low-lying area.

In spite of the fact that ancient walls show over the entire area of SFNW and SFW in places, especially central

Figure 18. Soccer Field West (SFW), looking northeast. Units 1 and 2 are in the foreground. The Abu Hol Sports Club is in the background on the right.

Mark Lehner

Figure 19. *Playa* deposits in the northwestern area of Soccer Field West, looking southeast. A reference section through the sandy overburden (dark horizontal band) can be seen in the background.

SFW, we see in the sides of pits that less than 20 cm, and sometimes just a few centimeters, of ancient walls and floors remain over a lower layer of clean sand upon which the builders founded the Western Town 4,500 years ago. Here and there we see exposed the floors of buildings, with absolutely no mudbrick tumble from the decay or collapse of the walls. There is more depth to the west, around Units 1 and 2 (fig. 18).

Upon such a settlement layer rests a small mastaba tomb, presumably built in the Old Kingdom (see fig. 20). The higher mudbrick core of this mastaba tomb has remained exposed since the 1980s, looking like a fragment of a mudbrick wall. Until we cleared it this season, we thought it was a wall of the settlement. But it turned out to be an outlier of the Workers' Cemetery up the slope. We say more about the implications of this tomb below.

Ponds and Pools: Northwest of the Soccer Field (SFNW)

Large stratified patches of gravelly sand, gravel, and *tafla* (desert marl clay) covered much of the area northwest of

the soccer field, just south of the big bend in the Enclosure Wall (fig. 19). Since these deposits presented a record of the site and the local environment after the Western Town had been abandoned, we did not want to simply remove them. The large *playa*-like patches consist of layers of intercalated sand and marl desert clay, and extend over an area 60 m south of the thick elbow in the Enclosure Wall to our grid line N99,000 and 35 m west of Enclosure E5. Where these post-occupational deposits do not cover the mud mass, alluvial mudbrick walls with marl plaster lines show clearly in the surface.

We are certain that standing pools of water left the *tafla* patches. The water naturally levigated the soil; that is, separated out the fine clay from sand and gravel. There are patches of *tafla* with large crack patterns, up to 25 cm between the cracks, such as one might see in gullies, gulches, wadis, and *arroyos* anywhere in the world (fig. 19). The post-occupational history of the site—what happened after the Pyramid Age settlement was abandoned—is important for understanding what forces and events left the site as we find it.

We left the large patches of naturally levigated clay. We also left long strips of sandy overburden; testimonial balks or reference sections of the deposits that covered the pond and pool deposits. Our longest balk stretches 45 m from the Enclosure Wall all the way to the little mastaba, founded upon the ruins of the Western Town (fig. 20). In this reference section, we even left the crushed limestone bed of the modern road to the Workers' Cemetery. The road ran over the north end of the tomb.

Tobias Tonner continued his investigation of post-occupation environmental history of the site by dissecting a dozen major layers of sand and *tafla* overlying the mud mass ruins of the ancient settlement. Joshua Trampier, Yukinori Kawae, and Lehner mapped Area SFNW.

Area of the Western Town

The mudbrick walls that show in between the sand, gravel and *tafla* patches in the area northwest of the soccer field are part of the ruins of the Western Town. These ruins cover an area 105 to 120 m north-south. This part of the city may have once extended across Lagoon 1 (fig. 20) and included the enclosures (ES1–2) on Standing Wall Island (see below), extending the Western Town nearly 200 m south of the Enclosure Wall around the Gallery Complex (see below). We have cleared and mapped the Western Town for a width of more than 60 m east-west, between the soccer field and the access road running between our site and the Workers' Cemetery up the slope. The town certainly extends under the road on the west, and under the Inspectors' rest house on the south-southwest, and probably underneath the lower part of the Workers' Cemetery.

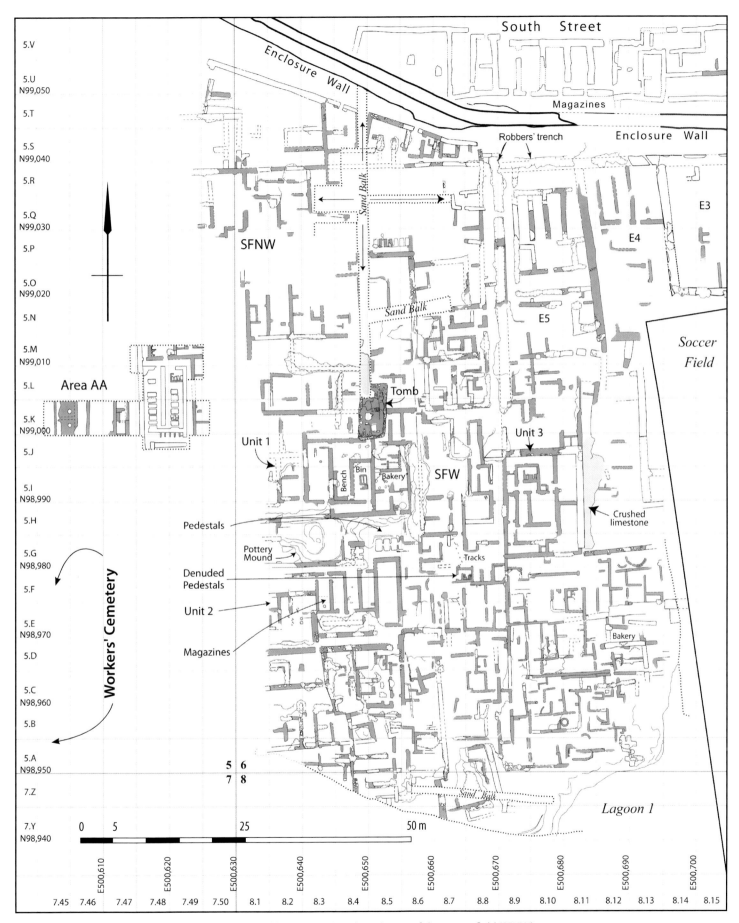

Figure 20. Plan of the Western Town, Areas Soccer Field West (SFW) and northwest of the soccer field (SFNW).

Nature of the Western Town

The overall ground plan of the Western Town (fig. 20) is the main prize of our long 2004 season.

Summarizing the work of the SFW team, Justine Gesell (Gesell et. al. 2004) wrote:

Extensive surface scraping, followed by shallow excavations revealed an expansive site with large scale architecture, occupying the area south of the Enclosure Wall.... When looking at the plan, four major units, marked by large mudbrick and/or limestone walls, become apparent:

The "bakeries" in the northwest

The magazines in the southwest

The house unit in the northeast

An enclosed area with smaller architecture, possibly "living quarters" in the southeast.

It is possible to divide SFW into an eastern, middle and western third, characterized by the different surfaces:

The eastern third of the site was underlying a thick layer of compact mud mass, which was covering walls and in some cases had obliterated the mudbricks.

The middle section was only underlying a layer of sand (especially ranges 6 and 7). The architecture was exposed at floor level, with little of the walls remaining. The walls and surfaces are very friable and slowly disintegrating. The ancient surfaces lay directly beneath the overburden of sand, with no evidence of tumble. It looks like this part of the site was swiped clean at one time.

The western third of the site is comprised of surfaces that are not as friable as the middle third, although the ancient architecture in the western third was also directly underlying the sand overburden.

Large Architectural Units in SFW

In the central part of SFW we distinguish three large rectangular units, corresponding to the "bakeries," "magazines," and "house unit," by the thickness of the outer walls (from 60 cm to 1 meter) and the length (up to 22 m) of these walls.

Unit 1

Unit 1, in the northwest part of SFW, includes the "bakeries" to which Gesell et. al. (2004) refers. This compound is 11.5 m north-south × 16 m east-west (measuring to the outsides of the walls) (fig. 20).

The "bakery" takes up the eastern end of the compound, measuring about 9.5 m north-south × 5 m east-west (measuring to the insides of walls). Thin walls divide this space into three parts. A doorway on the south leads to a small chamber in the southeast corner (2.3 × 2.6 m) filled with ashy material in which a circular patch might mark the position of a vat. The tops of jars show in the northeast corner of the chamber and in an accretion built into the southwest corner. Fragments of dolerite (used for hammers and grinders) lie near these jars and in a doorway to a small square chamber occupying the west part of the southern third of the "bakery." The middle third of the "bakery" is a chamber, 2.5 m north-south × 4.8 m east-west, in which several large fragments of limestone and granite, possibly grinding stones or querns, lie on the surface. The northern third of the "bakery" is a chamber 3.5 m square. There might be traces of thin walls in the fill. These could form compartments such as we saw at the southern back of the building in Area AA in 1991. The fill of these chambers is generally soft and very ashy, particularly in the chamber in the southeast corner.

Yukinori Kawae excavated a chamber in the middle part of Unit 1. The chamber is 8.5 m north-south × 5.70 m, measuring between the walls. In 22 cm of dry crumbly fill he found fragments of the roof that once covered this chamber: clumps of mud with impressions of reed and ropes (figs. 21, 22). Only traces remain of a wall that formed a room, 5.50 × 2.6 m (10 × 5 cubits) in the southeast corner of the larger rectangle. Out on the floor, standing free of the walls, he found a little magazine, 1.10 m north-south × 40 cm east-west, raised off the floor by thin plastered walls and divided into two compartments, each chockablock full of crude red ware pottery jars (fig. 23).

The chamber leaves an "L"-shaped space to the rest of the larger chamber, with the leg of the L to the west. A mudbrick bench graced the west and south sides of the upright part of the L. Black paint covered the remaining plaster along the bases of the walls of the chamber. South of the rectangular chamber in the center of Unit 1 is a corridor, unexcavated and filled with mud tumble, with one doorway opening to the bakery, and another into the room with the bin.

The back part of Unit 1 is another rectangular space, 8.5 m north-south × 3.5 m east-west. Black painted plaster covers the lower parts of the walls.

Unit 1 may very well continue farther west. There are indications that the south wall and corridor continue another 10 or 11 m farther west than we were able to positively map them. It is certain that marl-plastered mudbrick walls form a chamber attached to the south side of what we perceive as the west wall of Unit 1, extending the unit another 4 m west.

Unit 2

Unit 2, dubbed "the magazines" because of the four magazines on the north side of the compound, extends 13.5 m north-south and more than 22 m east-west (fig. 20). The west end of this unit cannot be determined as it runs past the limits of our clearing. There is possibly an entrance at the south end of the east side into a small vestibule, which then opens to a corridor running west. A trench at the north side of this space marks where someone removed a wall, probably to reuse the bricks (see below). This wall once screened the entrances to the two middle magazines. The magazines are about 5.2 m (10 cubits) long north-south and 1.6 to 1.8 m wide. The set of four reminds us of the four magazines in E5, the magazine complex northwest of the soccer field (see above). The magazines on both the east and west ends of the set of four open onto a corridor more than 15 m long and only 70 to 80 cm wide.

Pottery Mound: 1988 "Square A3"

The east end of the north corridor in Unit 2 opened north onto a rectangular area, 6.2 m wide, between Units 1 and 2 (fig. 20). Two of the curious sets of pedestals occupy this space, one set to the west, oriented north-south, and another to the east, oriented east-west. The west wall of this space retains a big mound of pottery sherds. Lehner has seen this mound of sherds exposed since the mid 1980s. In our first season, 1988, we laid out a square on this mound, which we designated A3 in our nomenclature of that time, but we never excavated it. The pottery mound appears to be a trash deposit, neatly contained between the walls of Units 1 and 2 (in Squares 6.H–G2–3). A clay sealing imprinted with Khafre's name came from surface cleaning in the southeast corner of the mound.

A large court or room takes up the eastern front of Unit 2, east of the magazines and north of the vestibule. The court is 9 m long (north-south) and 2.9 m wide (east-west).

Unit 3

Unit 3, "the house," would not be recognizable from the surface mapping if it were not for Justine Gesell's diligent excavations (fig. 20). Our impression going over this area is that the site was covered by settlement material pureed by water or moisture into a homogenous, light gray, sandy mud with scattered sherds. As Gesell et. al. (2004) report, even where we know the wall exists by virtue of the intact marl plaster lines, the bricks have dissolved into the homogenous gray with scattered sherds, something we have experienced in the northeast part of the Gallery Complex. Why the plaster remains, while the brick lines dissolve, may have something to do with water soaking up through the sand layer that covered the mudbrick walls. Nile floods that filled the nearby depression, Lagoon 1 (see

Yukinori Kawae

Mark Lehner

Figure 21. Top: fragment of roofing material from Unit 1.

Figure 22. Above: Yukinori Kawae holds a roofing fragment from Unit 1 in the Western Town. The mud chunks show impressions of reeds, rope, and matting.

below), could have provided the moisture that dissolved bricks and walls after people had abandoned the site.

Unit 3 is 16 m north-south and 12.3 m east-west. An entrance may have opened on the north end of the west side, where the walls are worn away. There are two small vestibules here, one after another leading from west to east into the house. A doorway on the left (north) of the second vestibule leads to a small chamber with a set of three pedestals on the south wall, and a doorway to the right (south) leads to a corridor and long rooms and magazines in the southwest corner of the house. A second doorway on the right opens in the northwest corner of a room, 4 m north-south × 3.5 m east-west, in the very center of the house. Two large rectangular chambers, just under 7 m long north-south and 2.5 to 2.8 m wide east-west, occupy the length of the east side of the house.

The eastern wall of Unit 3 stands out for its thickness, more than a meter, and because it is all fieldstone, while the other walls are predominately mudbrick. Between this wall and another fieldstone wall running parallel 8.8 m farther east very few walls show. A sheet of crushed limestone (fig. 20) gives this broad rectangular swath the appearance of a street. However, walls belonging to the

Enclosures 4 and 5 close this space off on the north, giving it a total length of about 30 m.

To the south of Unit 3, thinner walls, 30 to 60 cm thick, and an eastward continuation of the south wall of the house, enclose a rectangular space, 8.5 to 9.5 m wide north-south and more than 24 m long, extending farther east than the house itself. Thin walls subdivide this space into small chambers or compartments. Gesell et. al. (2004) referred to this area as "living quarters." Or, these could be support structures attached to Unit 3. Between here and the steep drop into Lagoon 1, there are many small walls defining more small chambers and some circular and curved walls that could be granary silos. One rectangular structure, about 6 m east-west × 4.5 m north-south, is most probably a bakery.

All of this—the hypothetical "street," the enclosure with small chambers on the south of Unit 3, and a myriad of small walls and chambers farther south to the Lagoon— pass under the west side of the soccer field.

Central SFW

The alignments of certain walls define a north-south central zone to central SFW. This includes the east walls

Figure 23. Workmen clear around a double bin (location shown on the map) filled with crude red ware pottery in Unit 1 of the Western Town.

of Units 1 and 2, although they are about a meter out of alignment (fig. 20). The east wall of Unit 2 aligns with another wall that continues 12 m farther south. These walls provide the west boundary to the central zone. The west wall of Unit 3, 16 m long, and a southerly continuation of this alignment by thinner walls another 18 m give the east boundary to the central zone. The central zone, thus defined, is 16 m wide east-west.

Many walls and bits of walls show on the surface, suggesting that this strip is divided into courts and chambers. Just about in the center, in Squares 6.F7–8, Mark Kincey excavated a small enclosure around a denuded version of the pedestal features. It is possible that these bits of walls belong to more large compounds that occupied the central zone and were contiguous with Units 1, 2, and 3. Or the courts and chambers in the central strip could be support structures for the large units that we have distinguished. We need to excavate further to clarify the ground plan of the central zone.

Small Structures in South SFW

Smaller structures extend south of central SFW and Units 1, 2, and 3 in an area 15 to 25 m north-south and 60 m east-west. Like the buildings in the Eastern Town, these structures are less oriented to the cardinal directions; they turn farther west of north. The small structures could be smaller residential units, as in the Eastern Town, although this part of the Western Town appears to be even more crowded. On the east-southeast of this area the settlement layer slopes down into the depression of Lagoon 1.

The east end of this southern zone was where it was most problematic to see the walls. Here the site had been wet, most probably by proximity to ground water in the nearby Lagoon 1. The deposits, while wet, were compressed and twisted, and then dried into swirl patterns.

Many pits mark the settlement remains on the west end of this southern zone for a stretch of 40 m higher up the slope. We think these pits date to ancient times, when people mined the settlement ruins for mudbrick (see below). Where the robbers left the brick, the walls are well-preserved. This part of the town passes under the substantial sandy overburden that remains immediately on the south and west. The access road and the inspectors' house for the Workers' Cemetery excavations rest on this overburden.

Other Large Units? Area AA of 1988–1991

Other large units like those in central SFW might lie to the north of Unit 1 in the area we designated SFNW. This is the area of gravel and *tafla* (marl desert clay) patches left by ponds of water. Because we did not excavate those patches, we do not see the total exposure of the ancient town walls in this area. Given the parts we could map,

the walls appear to be thicker and aligned to the cardinal directions like the walls around Units 1, 2, and 3.

Our excavations in Area AA during our first seasons, 1988–'89 and 1991, lie just up the slope from where we cleared in SFNW (fig. 20). The buildings we found in Area AA are certainly part of one of the orderly large units. The central building in AA, 9 m north-south long and 6 m wide, housed two rows of pedestals on either side of a central dividing wall. Immediately to the east we excavated the west part of a mudbrick building that looked domestic. This is certainly the same building whose walls we mapped this season in SFNW in Squares 6.K-L1, separated by only one 5 × 5-m square from the 1988–'89 excavation (then Square A1). We now know AA is part of the Western Town.

The large units appear to have occupied the area extending almost to the big bend in the Enclosure Wall around the Gallery Complex. The walls stop short of a corridor, just under 2 m wide, defined by a fieldstone and mudbrick wall, 70 cm to 1 m thick, running parallel to the Enclosure Wall at the angle of the big bend, about 18.5° north of due west. The corridor continues for more than 40 m at this angle.

The five enclosures, E1–5, west of the Royal Administrative Building could also be large house compounds. The enclosures, however, appear to be more strictly demarcated by extra thick fieldstone walls, like the enclosures in Standing Wall Island (see below).

Wall Robbing

A remarkable feature of the Western Town is the degree to which people robbed the walls of bricks and fieldstone. The trenching out of walls begins with the west wall of E5 and, even farther east, the wall around the silo court in the Royal Administrative Building.

Robbers' Trenches in the Western Town

Wall trenching increases to the southwest and accounts for the many pits in the western part of the southern zone of SFW. There are many examples where part of the wall remains in mudbrick, while a ragged trench follows the line of the rest of the wall. To capture the ground plan of the settlement, it became necessary to include in the overall, large-scale map the trenches and pits in addition to the parts of walls that remain. There are cases where the robbers took out the bricks so neatly that they left the marl plaster intact along the sides of the trench. In a few cases, the plaster still retains black paint (as in Unit 1, Square 6.I3). Then there are cases where the brick robbers emptied out a chamber (as in Square 6.N6), evidently finding usable bricks in the tumble of the walls.

This robbing happened before the sandy overburden covered the ruins.

Figure 24. In the Soccer Field West area workmen clear an Old Kingdom tomb, a possible outlier of the Workers' Cemetery nearby. The stones in the tomb were probably looted from the walls of the Western Town. The lines running under the tomb in the right foreground are marl plaster lines of settlement walls. View to the northeast.

Yukinori Kawae

Old Kingdom Mastaba on Western Town Ruins

Since our earliest season in 1988–'89 a mudbrick wall has been exposed in the area we now designate sFW. The sand diggers from the nearby riding stables probably uncovered this wall, which falls in our grid squares 6.K-L4–5. It measures about 2.80 m east-west and 4.70 m north-south. This wall and the mound of crushed pottery to the southwest (between Units 1 and 2) are two features that first suggested settlement remains of the Pyramid Age lay below this track of low desert.

After clearing down to the ancient surface, we saw that the wall is actually the core of a tomb (fig. 24), an extreme eastern outlier of those mudbrick and fieldstone tombs of the lower Workers' Cemetery excavated by the team of Dr. Zahi Hawass. Fieldstone walls increase the tomb dimensions by 1 m on the south and 50 cm wide on the east. Two shafts penetrate the mud core on the south. The shafts measure 0.80 × 1.00 m (west) and 0.90 m square (east). A third shaft, 1.20 m square, may lie to the north on the west side.

Chunks of mudbrick wall that still retain the plaster face lay in the compressed rubble layer of the ruins immediately in front of and slightly southwest of the tomb. These big pieces and others tell us something about how the settlement initially came down. The tomb rests directly upon the north wall of Unit 1 and the remains of marl-lined walls of what is probably another large (house)

structure farther north. The settlement ruins were already in the condition in which we found them when the tomb was built, presumably in the later Old Kingdom.

The situation of the tomb is reminiscent of the stone-built section of the wall between the first and second galleries to the west in Gallery Set IV (IV.1, IV.2). Mohsen Kamel cleared and mapped that wall in 2000. The stone section had stood long after the rest of the wall, built in mudbrick, had melted away. When the stone section finally collapsed, the stones tumbled down onto a mud mass eroded to the level at which we found it. Powerful forces of erosion had formed the surface of the mud mass and its contours before the stones fell and rolled onto the surface that we scrape to find the outlines of walls. So it is here, in sFW. The remains of the settlement were already cut down to the level at which we find them before someone built this little tomb.

If the tomb was built in the Old Kingdom, powerful forces of erosion had already cleaved a horizontal section through our workers' city before the end of the Old Kingdom. If the tomb is 5th Dynasty, the top of the city was blown away soon after the demise of the 4th Dynasty of Giza pyramid builders; that is, soon after the royal house moved away from Giza to Saqqara and Abu Sir.

These facts make it a very compelling hypothesis that the brick and fieldstone robbers who stripped the walls of the Western Town were the tomb builders of the later

Old Kingdom, and that many of the bricks in the tombs up the slope, as well as some of the broken stone—mostly limestone but also granite—derive from walls of the town below. For the severe reduction of the ruins in SFW, down to a few centimeters above the bottoms of walls and floors, the Old Kingdom tomb builders, in addition to natural forces of erosion, become likely suspects.

Lagoon 1

Lagoon 1 is a big depression where we lose the settlement. The surface sinks more than a meter lower than general floor level of the Western Town and nearly 3 m below soccer field grade. Our cut through the sand and overburden on which the soccer field is founded shows, from top down:

- 28 cm of modern cement, straw, plastic, brick, and paper
- a layer, 34 cm thick, of grayish brown, muddy sand with roots of the trees that line the soccer field
- a layer, 10 cm thick, of mud with modern inclusions, all soft clean sand down into and filling the Lagoon.

At its north end the Lagoon extends 22 m west of the soccer field and at its south end it extends more than 40 m west of the soccer field. The Lagoon fingers farther west than our clearing, passing under the thick modern overburden on which our new road to the Workers' Cemetery and our site now passes. North to south the Lagoon extends from our grid line N98,955 to N98,905, so about 50 m. It is a huge gap in the settlement.

We do not know the depth of the Lagoon. The settlement layer slopes gently to the east and dramatically to the southeast. We see just a bit of the depression running to the north before the Lagoon disappears under the soccer field section. Ground water quickly filled the depression at elevation 14.66 m asl. Where we excavated the sand deeper, the water pooled and the remaining sand was soft and saturated. The water level seemed to rise and fall daily. Over the months after we exposed it, the wet sand turned green with mold and started to sprout a variety of green plants.

Farther south, especially close to Standing Wall Island (see below), the sand diggers from the riding stables dug out the clean sand down to about the water table. People working for the stables then dumped the material from cleaning their stables into the excavated depression, and periodically burned the straw and chaff, leaving layers of black, powdery ash interspersed with layers of unburnt waste straw. The ash left a wet, black surface just at the water table. The soccer field already existed when the sand diggers dug the sand along the west of it, so the thick sand layer showing in our section under the soccer field along its west side corresponds roughly to the section

the sand diggers already created. The soccer field itself prevented them from digging the clean sand farther east, and therefore preserved much of the original sand cover. Whether this is the case all the way under the soccer field can only be determined when we are able to excavate in the field.

Is it possible that the Lagoon is an ancient feature? Or did forces of erosion cut this deep depression into the southern part of the site after the inhabitants abandoned the Western Town?

The settlement deposits on the north and west edges of the Lagoon, along the boundary with the Western Town, are comprised of extensive dumps of ashy pottery, like the dumps in Area EOG, east of the Gallery Complex, an area of bakeries and of the curious pedestals. Here we see structures that are almost certainly bakeries, close to the shore of the Lagoon, one showing prominently just south of the large house (Unit 3) close to the soccer field. These deposits might suggest that the Lagoon already existed as a depression when the people lived in the Western Town. The occupants may have located facilities that produced much refuse near this depression so that they could dump the waste in it, just as people nowadays dump garbage in canals.

Long rectilinear efflorescences of salt appear like winter frost on the wet sandy surface stretching up to 25 m north-northwest from Standing Wall Island across the southern part of the Lagoon (fig. 25). It is possible that the salt lines mark ancient walls or the spaces between walls that lie deeper in the fill of the Lagoon. The salt lines show about the same orientation as the walls on Standing Wall Island. In the Western Town ruins we have seen salt effloresce on walls, or on the debris fill between walls, leaving a frosty outline of the architectural ground plan. Perhaps the settlement at one time continued across a slight depression that Nile floodwater subsequently eroded into the deeper Lagoon after the inhabitants abandoned the site.

Standing Wall Island (Southwest)

Moving south across the Lagoon to grid line 8.Q, the ancient settlement suddenly reappears (fig. 1). Ninety cm south of point 8.P13 we found the hard shoulder of a fieldstone wall that stood high, shrouded in black ash, straw, and bits of trash dumped by people from the riding stables. This shoulder turned out to be our first wall, other than the Wall of the Crow and the Enclosure Wall, standing above, as opposed to being flush with, the mud mass or fieldstone tumble. We dubbed it "Standing Wall."

Standing Wall forms the north side of a complex, 27 to 30 m east-west × 17.50 to 26 m north-south (fig. 25). This complex consists of two large compounds or enclosures, ES1 and ES2, that face south, opening at the edge of another depression, Lagoon 2, filled with sand down to the water

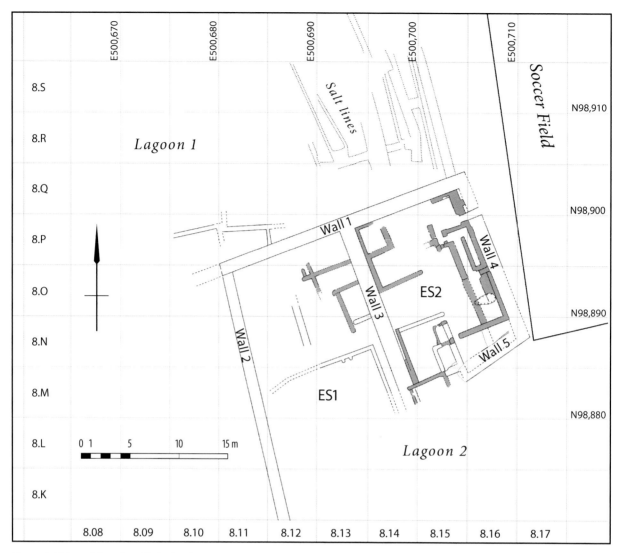

Figure 25. Plan of Standing Wall Island.

table. Standing Wall Island is the area of ES1 and ES2 bounded on the north by Lagoon 1 and on the south by Lagoon 2.

The Standing Wall Island compound is oriented markedly west of north at 21°, more than the deviation of the Gallery Complex, which is a little less than 3° west of north, and more than the western stretch of the Enclosure Wall around the Gallery Complex, which is about 12–13° west of north.

Standing Wall (Wall 1)

Standing Wall rises more than 1.50 m above the mud mass at its base and more than 2 m higher than the wet sand we left in Lagoon 1, whose southern shore is just off Standing Wall's northern base (figs. 25, 26). This is a fieldstone wall, 1.2 to 1.5 m wide, running east-west but at a pronounced angle north of east. The part of Standing Wall that stands above the surface runs 15 m to the west-southwest. At

that point another fieldstone wall runs south-southeast. Standing Wall runs farther west than this juncture, sloping down into the section, 1.50 m tall, that we cut through the overburden upon which passes our access road to the site from south to north. Here the overburden is sand, thick with straw; modern plastic; lower ash layers of burnt stable dumping; and at the bottom, 1 m to 30 cm of clean sand.

We certainly did not expect an ancient wall to project up into this very recent, modern material. The stable diggers, taking the clean, dry sand for cleaning the stable floors, must have excavated down and around Standing Wall. The wall must not have stood bare for very long—in any case, it went archaeologically unnoticed—before the stable folk returned the sand with its new inclusions and straw. They burned off some of the straw at the bottom of their sand pit and directly over the surface of Standing Wall, which they also reburied with straw and trash.

Figure 26. Workmen clean sand off "Standing Wall" at the south end of Soccer Field West (SFW). View to the southwest.

Recent Damage to Ancient Ruins

Our 2003 trench, sfw-s, came down onto the mud mass within enclosure es2 just east-southeast of Standing Wall (Lehner 2003: 67–68). Between the area we exposed in this trench and Lagoon 1, the ancient mud mass became mixed with modern ash, soot, and debris in a patch, 11.90 m east-west × 6.50 m north-south. Very ancient and very modern material got mixed when all the material was very wet, almost liquid, then dried into wavy patterns like television static. We found similar patterns in the ancient material elsewhere on the site, particularly in the northeast part of the Gallery Complex in 2000 and 2001. Marl plaster wall lines will run straight until they hit such a patch, then go wavy where the walls melted and solidified in their wavy pattern from drying. In this part of Standing Wall Island, the condition was more severe. The ancient material actually swirled all about and intermixed with modern material. The pattern of disturbance begins just where Standing Wall is truncated; that is, where someone chopped away the ancient wall.

The following sequence of events produced the swirled patch:

1. As the sand diggers removed the sand they found Standing Wall. They left the wall standing on the west, but removed it down to its foundations on the east, making a big pit between Standing Wall and the soccer field, which was already there when someone dug the pit. The soccer field preserved the clean sand underneath it. To the west of the pit,

the sand diggers did not dig lower than the top of Standing Wall. Between these areas, they scooped the sand down to the level of the mud mass, destroying Standing Wall down to its foundation.

2. People dumped trash and straw from stable cleaning into the pit. They periodically burned this material, mixing black ash and soot with modern glass, plastic, brick, and cement.

3. The water table rose from the Lagoon 1 depression immediately on the north and saturated the foundation of Standing Wall, the ancient mud mass deposits to the south (inside enclosure es2), and the modern material. Saturated modern material covered the mud mass and filled the interstices of the stones in the foundation of Standing Wall.

4. As we cleared the modern material, and what was left of the ancient sand, the weight of the loader and the feet of the workers, unfortunately, further intermixed the saturated ancient and modern deposits into the swirled patterns that "solidified" by drying soon after we exposed them.

Last year we just happened to sink our trench, sfw-s, through the modern stable dumping and some remaining clean sand, almost immediately south of the sand diggers' cut into the ancient material where they removed a good stretch of Standing Wall. So in 2003 we not only just missed Standing Wall (Wall 1) by a few meters, but we missed this modern pit through the ruins, and its fill of burnt trash down to the ruins, though we had it at a higher level over the clean sand layer that the pit diggers left.

Wall 2

Wall 2 attaches to Standing Wall, about 14.5 to 15 m from the truncated west end of Standing Wall (fig. 25). Wall 2 runs about 6.5° off of perpendicular to Standing Wall, and about 14° east of due south. Fieldstone that slumped off the top of Wall 2 obscures the edges, or faces, of this wall, but it appears to be 1.00 to 1.10 m thick. On the east side of Wall 2, the fieldstone that slumped off the wall forms a layer 30 to 40 cm thick that rests on sand. The workmen cleared the sand down below the level of this slump, leaving it on a "pedestal" of gray, silty sand 35 cm thick. On the east side of Wall 2 a cleaner, less silty sand lens, 12 cm thick, runs through the gray silty sand. Under the silty sand is a layer, about 15 cm thick, of clean sand down upon the surface of the mud mass that filled enclosure ES1. The silty sand/clean sand sequence occurs under the slump off the east side of Wall 2 for 12 m to the south of Standing Wall.

We cleared Wall 2 for a distance of 25 m south-southwest and it appears to continue farther under the sand and modern overburden. Here Wall 2 runs well past the northern edge of Lagoon 2.

On the west side of Wall 2 the situation is much messier. Here we have modern rubbish for a width of 8.7 m on the north and 9.5 m on the south in the space between Wall 2 and the section we cut through this very recently dumped stable straw, plastic bags, bottles, bricks, soot, and ash. Our access road curves around from the south and runs over this trash, 3 m west of the ragged section that our loaders left cutting through the trash.

Wall 3

The west face of Wall 3 is 11.70 (on the north end) to 13.70 m (on the south end) east of the east face of Wall 2 (fig. 25). Wall 3 attaches perpendicular to Standing Wall and runs 18.50 m south-southeast from Standing Wall where it ends abruptly at Lagoon 2. Wall 3 is 1.50 to 1.60 m wide. As of this writing, some of this thickness may be fieldstone slump off its sides. We have yet to ascertain the faces of the wall and know its true thickness. The west face of Wall 3 shows clearly, but the east face is ragged, disturbed. The same cut that truncated Standing Wall on the east took a triangular bite, 2.60 to 3 m wide, out of nearly the whole width of Wall 3 just 1.60 to 2 m south of Standing Wall. Someone took another bite, 2 m wide, out of the east face of Wall 3 at 8.50 to 10.50 m south of Standing Wall.

We first saw part of Wall 3 in our season 2003, at the western side of SFW-S, the southern of two trenches that we cut through the overburden down to the mud mass

(Lehner 2003: 67–68). Where Wall 3 attaches to Standing Wall, it also stands above the mud mass, nearly 1 m tall. It eroded southwards, sloping down to only 30 cm above the mud mass at its southern end.

Enclosure ES1

Standing Wall turned out to be the north side of two adjacent large enclosures, ES1 and ES2 (fig. 25). Walls 2 and 3 form the respective west sides of these southern enclosures. Standing Wall is about 30 cm thinner, at 1.20 m, where it forms the north boundary of ES1 than where it runs north of ES2.

Because of the westward angle of Wall 2, ES1 is a trapezoid that is narrower at the northern end, at 11.70 m, than at the southern end where it is almost 14 m.

Enclosure ES1 contains a mud mass of light brown, sandy silt that sinks down in the center about 1 m below the preserved tops of Walls 2 and 3. The dip is due to the erosion of mudbrick walls that divide the space of ES1.

Yukinori Kawae supervised the workmen who cleaned ES1 at the end of the season. He mapped traces of mudbrick walls along the west side of Wall 3, which separates ES1 from ES2. He also mapped a thin fieldstone wall that runs parallel to the south end of Wall 3, then turns 90° to run west, closing off ES1 about 11.5 m from the north wall (Standing Wall) (fig. 25). He saw in the mud mass traces of a thicker fieldstone wall running north-south and dividing the enclosed area in half.

Tumbled and eroded alluvial and marl mudbrick rises in the corner formed by the west face of Wall 3 and Standing Wall. The slightly mounded mudbrick tumble spreads out 70 cm to 1.40 m along the south face of Standing Wall. From the south face of Standing Wall the mud mass slopes down slightly to the south for a distance of 12.50 m, then drops precipitously into Lagoon 2. Walls 2 and 3 extend another 5.5 m farther south than the drop off of the mud mass.

Enclosure ES2

Because the southern wall (Wall 5) of ES2 runs at an angle south of west (see below), ES2 is also a trapezoid, about 15 m long (north-south) on the east and 18.50 m long on the west. The east and west walls of ES2, that is Walls 3 and 4, are parallel, making this enclosure a consistent 11.20 m wide (fig. 25).

The north wall of ES2 is Standing Wall, taken down to its foundation where it runs east of Wall 3, separating ES1 from ES2. The east wall of ES2 is only partly exposed from where it runs under the west side of the soccer field. It is fieldstone, from 1.20 to 1.30 m thick, and runs for about 16 m where it makes a corner with a thick fieldstone wall (Wall 5) that runs west-southwest to close off ES2 on the south. We are not certain of the thickness of Wall 4, but it could be thicker, at 1.60 to 1.70 m, than the other fieldstone walls in ES1 and ES2.

The corner of Walls 4–5 is not certain, and sits within a mass of fieldstone that is mostly buried in the clean sand and overburden under the southwest corner of the soccer field. Wall 5 is not perpendicular to Wall 4, but runs at an obtuse angle 35° south of west for about 8 m. It appears that some length was removed from the original west end of Wall 5. The original south face of Wall 5 is well preserved and drops straight down into the depression of Lagoon 2 at a slight batter or slope.

The fieldstone walls defining ES2 were built up and around an older mudbrick complex. This is clear from the southwest corner of ES2, where two thin mudbrick walls of the earlier structures are embedded within the thick end of Wall 3. When they made Wall 3, the builders simply packed the fieldstone all round the thinner mudbrick walls. On the east, hard against the section of overburden along the soccer field, the mudbrick walls of the older complex run directly against the west side of Wall 4. It appears that the builders erected Wall 4 in fieldstone up against the thinner and older mudbrick walls.

The fact that Wall 5 ends 4.5 m short of meeting the west wall of ES2 (Wall 3) leaves a wide opening to the south. A short stub of fieldstone wall, continued by a thin mudbrick wall, closed this opening. There may be an entrance through this wall, but this is not certain. The thin mudbrick wall belongs to a rectangular court, 5.20 m (10 cubits) north-south × 4.30 m east-west. The west wall of this court is mudbrick, running directly alongside the fieldstone of Wall 3. There is a small compartment (1.3 × 2 m) in the southeast corner of the court. Immediately north of this compartment, a slight rise in the mud mass, 1.8 × 1 m, might mark a small (sleeping?) platform or bench, such as we have found in houses elsewhere on the site. A doorway opens in the far north end of the east wall of this court (or house?).

We see in the mud mass fill of ES2, the southern and western mudbrick walls, 40–50 cm thick, possibly belonging to another court or structure about 6.5 m north-south × 5 m east-west.

A more complex and problematic pattern of mudbrick walls shows in the mud mass against the east wall of ES2. The pattern is made less clear by the brick collapse or tumble of the mudbrick walls, which appear to have stood quite high against Wall 4. Damage caused by loaders, and the mixing and swirling of ancient and modern material at the lower, northern end of this side of ES2 also helped to obscure the pattern. Those who dug away the east end of Standing Wall and made the big pit near the northeast corner of ES2 removed the upper parts of these mudbrick walls and mudbrick tumble.

The walls along the east of ES2 appear to form a kind of zigzag entrance into a corridor, 9.5 m long and only 80 cm to 1 m wide, running northwest-southeast parallel to the east wall (Wall 4) of ES2. At the approximate center of the corridor, on the east side, a niche recedes to a small passage or doorway, half a meter wide, that opens to the east. Someone closed off this doorway with mudbrick. The fieldstone of Wall 4 additionally sealed the doorway. Another entrance at the south end of the corridor gave access to a narrow magazine, 4 m long and half a meter wide.

The zigzag entrance into the corridor and magazine departs from a small court in the very northeast corner of ES2. Standing Wall and Wall 4 form two sides of this court. Before those fieldstone walls had been built, mudbrick walls, 50 to 80 cm thick, defined the corner. Again, the builders raised the fieldstone walls directly against the earlier mudbrick walls. Here they left open an original passage or doorway through the mudbrick walls and continued it through the fieldstone of Wall 4. This leads to some space or structure as yet buried under the southwest corner of the soccer field.

In ES2 we see a pattern of thick fieldstone walls enclosing and fortifying an earlier mudbrick complex. Ana Tavares, Astrid Huser, Freya Sadarangani, and James Taylor found a similar sequence in their excavations of the northwest corner of the Royal Administrative Building where thick double fieldstone walls fortify and enclose an earlier mudbrick complex.

Lagoon 2

Lagoon 2 is another falling away of the site into a deep depression filled with sand to a depth below the water table (fig. 25). The depression extends farther south than the southern limit of our clearing this season, more than 15 m south of the southeast corner of ES1. Lagoon 2 is more than 28 m wide.

Dating the Lagoons

Are these depressions, Lagoons 1 and 2, ancient topographical features that existed during the 4th Dynasty occupation of the settlement, or are they post-occupation erosion features that took away parts of the ancient settlement? The following factors must be considered:

The settlement along the north rim of Lagoon 1 seems to include bakeries or other chambers for ash-producing industry. Where the settlement layer slopes down into the lagoon it contains much ash and pottery. This could suggest the depression already existed during the time of the occupation and served as a convenient dump.

The southern complex of two large enclosures, ES1 and ES2, could be imagined as referencing the depressions on either end of it, Lagoon 1 to the north and Lagoon 2 to the south, as though the lagoons, and, therefore, the high ground—the "island"—existed when the inhabitants built this complex (see fig. 1). The north wall of the complex (Standing Wall) roughly parallels the south edge of Lagoon 1. The south face of Wall 5, which partially blocks off enclosure ES2 on the south, is a sheer drop down into the wet sand filling Lagoon 2, again suggesting the depression was there when the wall was made.

The fact that the walls of the enclosures stand (or stood until very recent times) so high above the general mud mass, while the Lagoons drop so low immediately beside them, might suggest the depressions predate the walls.

Certainly the Lagoons predate the soccer field, for Lagoon 1 continued underneath the sports club. They also predate the clean sand layers that filled their depressions and blanketed the general site.

The Lagoons and Nile Floods

In certain old photos that show the site during flood season from various angles (unfortunately from afar) the inundation waters reach up to our site, some distance south of the Wall of the Crow, but as far west as the end of the Wall of the Crow. The water appears to fill depressions that finger westward in two places that might correspond with our Lagoon 1 and Lagoon 2.

There are these possibilities:

1. The ancient settlement continued into the depressions at a lower level just like other settlements that follow natural contours so there is no need to see forces of erosion as initially creating the lagoon.

2. Earlier settlement existed at a low level and forces of erosion cut into higher/later levels of settlement (there is no evidence yet of deeper, earlier phases of settlement in SFW).

3. The depressions are natural topographic features respected in ancient times (perhaps used for dumping) and later filled with floodwater as the flood plain rose and the inundation water reached farther west.

4. North of the Wall of the Crow

We carried out massive efforts north of the Wall of the Crow for nearly four months in our 2004 season (figs. 1, 27). When we began, modern trash and sand filled the whole area between the Wall of the Crow and a wall of cement and stone on the north that formed the southern boundary of the bus parking lot for visitors to the Sphinx and Khafre Valley Temple. A thick layer of modern garbage laid down in the late 1980s and early 1990s capped the fill, high onto the south side of the Crow Wall.

We removed the cement wall of the parking lot, and Mohammed Musilhi used the front-end loader to clear a 35 m-wide strip north-south, expanded to 40 m in the last week of the season, down to clean sand, from the east end of the Wall to the Great Gate, a distance of 105 m (200 cubits).

The Recent Historical Context of Our Clearing

Our clearing north of the Wall of the Crow involves the politics and history of the site since the 1980s to the present day. In the late 1980s, the area of the tourist bus parking lot, about 35 to 40 m north of the Wall of the Crow, was the storage yard for materials and equipment and the location of temporary field offices of AMBRIC, the British-American consortium, for their work installing a sewage system for the entire urban sprawl along the base of the Giza Plateau as part of the greater Cairo West Bank Waste Water Management Project. As the AMBRIC project wound down in the early 1990s, the area immediately north of the Wall of the Crow became a receptacle for modern trash that

Mark Lehner

Figure 27. North of the Wall of the Crow (WCN). Clearing deep overburden between the Wall of the Crow and the tourist bus parking lot, viewed from the top of the wall, looking northwest.

accumulated to a point, in the late 1990s, where we could no longer drive our Jeep through the Gate in the wall, as we had done in our 1991 field season. Eventually the broad area between the Wall of the Crow and the Sound and Light buildings to the north was leveled and graded for parking for tourist and school busses (fig. 28).

In 2001, we cleared the sandy overburden along the south side of the Wall of the Crow, through the Gate, and in a 5 × 5-m patch just beyond the north side of the Gate (Lehner 2001). We used sandbags to retain the sand and modern trash towering up to 4 m higher than the ancient road bed we exposed running through the Gate. At the end of that season, we back-filled the Gate and the excavation outside and north of it, so that camel and horse riders, visitors, and mourners attending funerals could once again cross the Wall through the Gate.

When we arrived in early January 2004, we found a construction project in full swing to build a high security wall all around both the Coptic Cemetery, south of the Wall of the Crow, and the larger Muslim Cemetery that once occupied the area north of the Wall of the Crow, but which has expanded in recent years up against the west and south sides of the red brick wall around the Coptic Cemetery, ascending the bank of debris up against the face of the prominent knoll of the Maadi Formation (the *Gebel el-Qibli*) (fig. 28). We were informed that this new high security wall is meant to contain the expansion of the modern cemeteries once and for all. It is also part of a plan, like the high security wall along the east of our site, to completely seal off the archeological and tourist area of the Giza Pyramids from the areas with modern life and housing.

We were informed that this plan calls for a corridor from the town to the Muslim and Coptic Cemeteries located within the heart of the archaeological zone. The corridor will be sealed by high cement and steel mesh walls like that along the east side of our site, all around the Giza Plateau, and like the wall around the modern cemeteries under construction during our 2004 season. As it stands now, people attending funerals must make their way to either the Muslim or Coptic Cemeteries down a street leading west at the north side of the bus parking lot, while tourist busses enter the parking lot, sometimes four or five back to back, on a cross street leading south, with many jams of vehicles, pedestrians, tourists, and sometimes funerals. This is not an acceptable situation.

We were told that the planned corridor will leave from a gate in the new high security wall, where it turns a corner after heading west, then north, at the southeast corner of the bus parking and north of the east end of the Wall of the Crow. The new corridor will lead west, parallel to the Wall of the Crow. The question was how far the new corridor should be from the north of the Wall of the Crow. At a point approximately on line with the north side of the Great Gate, the corridor will turn, and lead north to the entrance to the Muslim Cemetery. But the Coptic Cemetery entrance is south of the Wall of the Crow, through the Gate (fig. 28). Sealing off all local traffic from controlled visitor traffic would require an extension of the corridor onto the Gate itself, and continuing from the south side of the Gate to the Coptic Cemetery entrance south of it. This part of the corridor could be fencing of some kind rather than the solid cement and steel mesh, but it would nonetheless seal off the Gate.

With our concession to clear north of the Wall of the Crow this season, we had the opportunity to work with Dr. Zahi Hawass, Chairman of the Supreme Council of Antiquities, Sabry Abd el-Aziz, Director of Pharaonic Monuments, Mansour Boraik, Chief Inspector of Giza, Mohammed Shiha, our inspector, and the other authorities for the benefit of the archaeological interests that are at stake. They encouraged us to work quickly, again in salvage mode, to check the archaeology north of the Wall of the Crow, to expose the north face of the great Wall, and to help them decide about how to manage the difficult situation.

After we removed the overburden down to clean sand and exposed and cleaned the northern face of the giant Wall of the Crow, towering 8.8 m, everyone was encouraged to move the corridor as far as possible to the north, away from the Wall of the Crow. A compromise to which all agreed was to install the corridor below the grade of the bus parking, against the section through modern deposits that Mohammed Musilhi cut in order to reach the clean sand just over the hard ancient surface. Visitors at the higher level of the bus parking lot will then be able to look upon the Wall of the Crow and turn round to see a panorama of all three Giza Pyramids. Funerals could pass below, through the corridor, yet on a layer of protective sand above the compact ancient surface.

Below we discuss the archaeology of the operations we carried out north of the Wall of the Crow.

Archaeological Context North of the Wall of the Crow

The area north of the Wall of the Crow is archaeological *terra incognita*. It is the opening, some 200 m wide, of the wadi between the Moqattam limestone formation, the pyramids plateau proper, and the Maadi Formation, which is the escarpment rising west of our site (fig. 28). This broad area is filled with the expansive modern Muslim Cemetery to the west, just left of the northern exit through the Great Gate. To the north of the Wall of the Crow is the modern parking lot for busses that bring

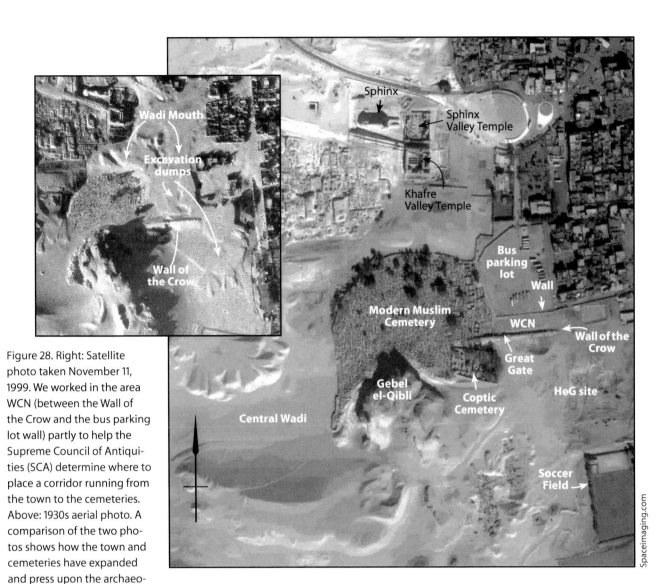

Figure 28. Right: Satellite photo taken November 11, 1999. We worked in the area WCN (between the Wall of the Crow and the bus parking lot wall) partly to help the Supreme Council of Antiquities (SCA) determine where to place a corridor running from the town to the cemeteries. Above: 1930s aerial photo. A comparison of the two photos shows how the town and cemeteries have expanded and press upon the archaeological zone.

Spaceimaging.com

tourists to visit the Sphinx and Khafre Valley Temple. Farther north the Sound and Light complex, seating area, and cafeteria face the Sphinx, Sphinx Temple, and the Khafre Valley Temple. In the Old Kingdom this broad area might have been the major access up into the Giza Necropolis.

Sand Layers in the Overburden North of the Wall

Using the loader, Mohammed Musilhi's team from the SCA Engineering Department cleared a strip 35 m wide (north to south) and removed the upper layers of trash dumped in the late 1980s and 1990s. Three large SCA dump trucks hauled the material away. Under the recent trash, the team removed gray sand with modern inclusions, the same or similar layers that we cleared from the eastern end of the Wall of the Crow in 2001 and 2002. The next

lowest sand layer has more limestone chips and flakes, and some Roman pottery such as amphorae fragments, but still modern inclusions. These layers showed many striations, or tip lines, from repeated dumping, likely from Selim Hassan's clearing in the Sphinx area during the 1930s. Tobias Tonner recorded some of these sandy layers in 2002 in Area WCE (in front of the east end of the Wall) (Tonner 2002). In the thick upper sand layers there we found modern inclusions down to the lowest very clean sand.

North of the Wall of the Crow the limestone chips and flakes of the next lowest layer, 1.50 m thick, are exfoliated from the large, but rather irregularly shaped blocks of the Wall of the Crow. The lowest layer over the Old Kingdom surface is extremely fine, clean sand. We did not find the limestone chip-filled sand that lay above the compact surface found in the square just beyond the north side of the Gate in 2001 (the layer contained many alabaster fragments, including very small fragments of statues and finished surfaces with a few carved hieroglyphs). Instead, the fine sand, about 1.40 m thick, lies directly upon the ancient, almost assuredly Old Kingdom surface.

The thickest overburden consisting of the combined layers was about 6 m in depth, nearly 7 m in operation WCGN in front of the Gate (see below).

Trench WCN

By the end of February, the workers, under the direction of Mohsen Kamel, had excavated a trench into the clean sand layer down to an Old Kingdom surface (figs. 1, 29). The trench was located 50 m west of the east end of the Wall, or 45 m east of the Gate (WCN). The original trench was 11 m wide and extended from the base of the Wall of the Crow for 15 m north.

Under the clean sand we found a thin layer of compact brown sand. This covered a compact surface composed of yellow *tafla* (marl, calcareous desert clay), crushed limestone from the Maadi Formation, and light brown sandy silt. It contained fragments of granite and patches of granite dust, recalling the strata of granite dust we found in similar fill on the south side of the Great Gate

in 2001 and the masses of granite dust filling a depression cut through Gallery Set I off the east end of the Wall of the Crow (WCE) in 2002 (Lehner 2002: 48–51). The material included Old Kingdom pottery fragments, bits of charcoal, some granite, and alabaster. We extended the trench more than 24 m north of the Wall where the compact surface continued sloping gently northward.

The compact surface north of the Wall is similar to the surface of marly limestone debris banked against the south side of the Wall of the Crow (WCS). Paul Sharman and Fiona Baker supervised clearing and excavating that surface in 2001 over a 15 × 75-m stretch (Sharman 2003). A deep trench up to the southern side of the Wall, nearly opposite our trench WCN this season, revealed that the compact surface on the south was the top of a massive deposit of limestone chips and *tafla*. It seemed that the builders left this against the Wall to make it even more dike-like than its 1:1 ratio of base width to height (10 m wide and 10 m tall). As we found in 2001, the path sloping down more than 2 m from south to north through the Gate was worn upon such deposits.

The surface is similar in the WCN trench but much lower. The Wall rises 8.80 m above it, whereas only 7 m of the Wall rises above the debris on the south side. If, as we

Figure 29. The Wall of the Crow North (WCN) trench viewed from the tourist bus parking lot. Mohsen Kamel (foreground) mapping with a Total Station. The Wall of the Crow towers above the trench.

saw in the WCS deep trench, the total height of the Wall is around 10 m, we should be only 1.20 m above the base of the Wall.

A wall composed of limestone fragments and gypsum runs 1.80 m north of and parallel to the Wall of the Crow. This might be part of a construction ramp sloping up to the mound banked against the north side, east end of the Wall of the Crow.

Masons' Mound: An Ancient Ramp?

In 2002 as part of our operation WCE (Wall of the Crow East), Lauren Bruning (2003) cleared part of a mound of crushed limestone and limestone fragments that we called the "Masons' Mound." This deposit is banked up against the north side of the Wall of the Crow at its eastern end. The builders appear to have left it when they stopped work on the upper courses of the Wall.

The mound rises about 3 to 4 m above the surrounding ancient surface about 10 m west of the east end of the great wall. The mound is composed of hard, compacted limestone debris with fragments of *tafla* and other rock from the Maadi Formation. This material looks very similar to that banked against the south side of the Wall of the Crow and the material filling the bottom of the Gate.

Bruning cleared the east side of the mound in 2002. We cleared the rest of the sand from the top of Masons' Mound this 2004 season. We also took out the layer of clean sand between the top of the mound and the WCN trench, 50 m west of the east end of the Wall. The compacted debris surface is continuous with the surface we found in that trench, a surface that probably extends all the way to the Gate, being the same as the compact surface in WCGN (see below). This surface extends at least 25 to 30 m north of the Wall of the Crow. In 2002 Bruning found the same or similar surface farther east, in her north-south trench, 15 m long, north of the east end of the Wall of the Crow (WCE).

At the top of Masons' Mound, beginning about 16 m west of the east end of the Wall of the Crow, there is a band of material that is distinguished from the masonry debris comprising most of the mound. This band, 11 m long and 2 m wide, is directly against the Wall, and filled with darker material that includes hard black stone, dolerite, alabaster fragments, bone, and much pottery. A disintegrated fieldstone wall may define the northern edge of the strip. This wall might relate to the limestone wall, 1.50 m wide, in the WCN trench running parallel to the Wall of the Crow about 40 m to the west.

The walls are embedded in the compact masonry debris. These walls could be the retaining walls of a ramp that sloped up eastward against the north face of the Wall of the Crow. Masons' Mound might be the remains of a debris-filled ramp that the workers left where they were moving stones up to work on the east end of the Wall of the Crow.

Operation WCGN: North of the Gate in the Wall of the Crow

Late into the Season 2004 we undertook a massive operation north of the Gate in the Wall of the Crow. The planned corridor to the modern cemeteries would occupy this area and turn to branch off to the Muslim Cemetery to the north and to the Coptic Cemetery to the south, through the Gate. With the encouragement of Mansour Boraik, Chief Inspector of the Giza Pyramids Inspectorate, and our senior SCA Inspector, Mohammed Shiha, we seized the opportunity to excavate directly in front of the Gate, and farther north than anyone had excavated, before the modern construction closed this option (figs. 1, 30).

Excavating down to the ancient surface was possible here only because of our enormous investment earlier in the season in clearing the general area. Our clearing left the overburden sloping down from west to east because the modern path through the Gate to the Coptic Cemetery remained at the higher level, descending from the bus parking lot, and because Mohammed Musilhi and our trucks needed a way up and down to clear, load, and haul the sandy overburden away.

We knew where to expect the level of the ancient surface based on the 5 × 5-m excavation square beyond the north side of the Gate in 2001 and from our clearing in the WCN trench.

Retrospective: North of the Gate in 2001

In 2001 we found what seemed to be stone builders' waste up against much of the length of the south side of the Wall of the Crow from the Gate to the east end. This compact debris consisted of compressed limestone, sand, and *tafla* clay with rings and pockets of granite dust. The debris filled the bottom of the tunnel through the Gate, sloping down to the north. Inside the tunnel, a thin deposit of brown, sandy soil with a fair amount of pottery overlay the masons' debris.

In a small probe trench against the east side of the passage, or tunnel, through the Gate, Baker found a series of five distinct use-surfaces (Sharman 2003). The latest surface was a delicate yellow, water-laid *tafla*. At elevation 16.30 asl, Baker found a cut through limestone rubble layers that must mark the trench for the foundation of the wall, though the probe did not actually reveal the bottom of the lowest block.

Our 2001 excavation, 5 m outside the Gate on the north, was at the bottom of a 4-m deep, sandbagged crater that we cleared through very recent trash, dirty sand and refuse, and then the clean sand.

In the clean sand layer we found pottery ranging from the 18th Dynasty blue-painted ware typical of the period of Akhenaten to impressed ware probably much later in date. This season we found more Amarna blue-painted pottery in clean sand that lay close to, or filled niches in, the lower north face of the Wall where blocks had been removed or fallen out. Close to the wall, a sand layer, about half a meter thick, contained scattered limestone chips that probably eroded off the Wall. We found the same or a similar chip layer as we cleared the lower part of the north face of the Wall to the east of the Gate this season.

Under the clean sand in the 2001 excavation north of the Gate, we exposed sand with limestone flecks [3705], 32 cm thick. This layer contained fragments of Egyptian alabaster with worked faces. Baker had the deposit sieved and picked over very carefully. Altogether, in just 8 cubic m of this sand, we recovered 1,450 alabaster fragments (30.5 kilograms), 103 with worked faces (2.1 kilograms). Among these were pieces with carved relief and a residue of copper inlay or green pigment; four fragments of a pleated wig or skirt (probably a wig); three fragments with scant edges of hieroglyphs, including one with an *f* (horned viper) and an *r* (mouth); and a small, nicely carved alabaster toe. We also sorted 100 kilograms of granite from this deposit. Many pieces look like chips from dressing granite with a pick.

Underneath the gravely sand, Baker came upon a layer, 5 cm thick, 70% compressed and rounded pottery sherds in brown sand [3706]. She believed that these had been trampled and washed by water. This surface slopes down to the north, continuing the slope of the *tafla/*limestone debris through the tunnel of the Gate. In fact the surface showed little runnels carved by water running away from the Gate. Under this was another use-surface, more compact, but also comprised to a great extent of trampled, worn ceramic fragments. This is probably quite thin above the same compact limestone rubble and debris that is mounded up outside the Gate on the south, and that forms the slope down to the north through the tunnel. The path across the crushed ceramic surface has a subtle camber—a convexity characteristic of ancient roadways in other contexts, where the sides slope away from the central path.

In 2002 Serena Love carried out a core drilling some 30 m north of the Gate through several meters of modern

Figure 30. The thumb-shaped clearing operation north of the Wall of the Crow's Great Gate (WCGN). Looking from the top of the wall to the northwest. The Muslim Cemetery is visible behind the clearing.

debris and then clean sand—a sequence similar to what we found in the excavations 5 m north of the Gate. The core drilling went through lower layers of silty sand with pottery sherds and then hard limestone debris.

The WCGN Pit and Upper Layers

In 2001 we backfilled our funnel-shaped pit down to the excavation square immediately in front of the Gate. In 2004 our objective in Operation WCGN was to clear down to the ancient surface as far north as possible on line with the Gate. Work began April 18, 2004, and closed May 19, 2004. Mohammed Musilhi's loader began, and Reis Ahmed Abd el-Basat's workers finished, an irregularly shaped, 7 m-deep cut, under Field Director Mohsen Kamel's supervision (fig. 30).

It was late into the season, well past our planned late-March deadline for intensive excavation, and most of the excavators had left. Fortunately Adel Kelany could stay and take on intensive investigation and documentation of the ancient deposits (Kelany 2004). Fatma Ali and Hanan Mahmoud assisted Kelany and did fine jobs mapping and drawing the sections of the excavation trenches. This team worked long hours in the heat of late April and May, when the sun reflected hot off the north side of the Wall of the Crow and off the bright ancient surface at the bottom of the sandy crater.

We cleared down to the ancient surface, generally around elevation 16.30 m asl, in the E-F-G tiers and the 34 and 35 ranges in Grid 1, starting 10 m north of the Wall of the Crow (fig. 1). Our exposure swung west to take in the east parts of Squares G-H-I 33. We left a ramp that descended from above the north edge of the exposure to the lower levels on the east of our cleared pit. The pit ended up with rounded, sloping sides that in a plan-view took the shape of a thumb bent to the west (fig. 30).

The upper edge of our cut began 6.20 m north of the north side of the Wall of the Crow, on line with the east side of the Gate. The cut went through modern dumping [4204] and then a thick layer of clean windblown sand [4205], such as we found over much of the area north of the Wall of the Crow under modern trash and old excavation dumps. The windblown sand [4205] is loose and contains occasional New Kingdom pottery sherds, some with blue-painted decoration, such as we found in the clean sand layer in the 2001 excavation, and near and in the north face of the Wall of the Crow this season. The windblown sand layer [4205] covered the whole area of Operation WCGN and the entire area along the Wall of the Crow for a distance of 40 m to the north.

Under the soft sand [4205] the team excavated a compact sandy layer [4206] that contained a moderate amount of pottery sherds, limestone cobbles and pebbles, and occasional sub-angular granite cobbles and pebbles.

This must be the same layer that contained the many alabaster fragments, some with bits of hieroglyphs, and fragments of small statues in the 2001 excavation square. We did find more granite fragments, but we did not find so much alabaster and none with worked faces. This material must have been confined to the area immediately in front of the Gate. In the southeast corner of our 2004 operation, in Square 1.E36, the team found animal footprints [4615] on the top of the compact sandy layer [4206].

The Old Kingdom Surface in WCGN

The softness of the sandy overburden meant we had to leave a slope as we went down. The slope took up about 4 m, so our ancient surface first appeared about 10 m north of the Wall, 5 m farther north than our exposure in 2001. Our exposed patch of ancient surface measured 17.50 m north to south on the west side, 15 m north to south on the east side, and about 13.20 m east to west across the base of the "thumb."

The Old Kingdom surface over the whole of our exposure is relatively flat and compact, beige to gray in color, with scattered pottery sherds. The surface is practically cemented, apparently from being wet and then drying. It is similar to the "masons' debris" against the south side of the Wall of the Crow, but here, beyond the north side of the Gate, the same material is flat and uniform. In spite of the nearly level uniformity of the surface, it is mottled in color, texture, and material, including ashy deposits, crushed limestone, gypsum, and granite dust. In Square 1.G34 there is a patch of smooth, compact *tafla* and a reddish patch of crushed pottery shards.

Mudbrick Lines

In spite of the patches and mottling, there is almost nothing structural about this surface: no roadway, no edge, no alignment with the Gate, no obvious camber or way. The only exceptions are two parallel lines of alluvial mudbrick, 1.68 m apart, in Square 1.F32, off to the east-northeast from an alignment with the Gate. The brick lines are oriented northeast-southwest and curve slightly. The west line [4233] is 3.40 m long. It extends slightly farther south than the east line. The east line [4232] is about 3 m long, formed of bricks 16 cm wide and 26 to 27 cm long. Our excavation through the southern end of the two brick lines reveals that only a centimeter or less remains of the bricks set into, and upon, coarse reddish sand [4234] with scattered sherds. The surface of this reddish material spreads between and around the two brick lines.

The double brick-line feature points roughly toward the Gate. Just beyond it to the south, in the direction of the Gate, lies a patch of ashy material containing large, very worn, pottery sherds. We exposed this patch after peeling back the compact coarse sand [4206] that appears to have been cemented (or calcified) by water soaking. (The soft sand with Amarna blue-painted pottery [4205] overlay the cemented sand).

The double brick line might be the continuation of what we thought was a cambered way, covered with crushed or very worn pottery fragments that we exposed immediately outside the Gate on the north in 2001. The double brick lines end about 15 m short of the Gate, or 10 m shy of the 2001 square (1.C34), and northeast of it.

It is hard to see a purpose for the brick-lined path. The bricks are too thin to have been parts of substantial walls that might have formed a corridor. The brick lines seem, anyway, to be a very thin residue of a structure most of which eroded away, perhaps washed away by water, for there is unequivocal evidence that the whole surrounding surface was very wet at one time, if not repeatedly so.

Animal Tracks

We had the impression in 2001 that the debris banked up against the south side of the Gate was cemented by having been wet. Stratified use-surfaces inside the gate also appear to have been water soaked. Animal footprints in the hard, compact surface north of the Gate in WCGN leave little doubt that this surface too was once soft and wet.

The animal footprints are concentrated in the southeast part of the exposure, particularly in Squares 1.F34 and 1.G34, which is to say on line with the Gate. We tracked about 28 imprints that appear to have been made by hooves. Our faunal specialist, Richard Redding (2004), thought that cattle made some.

Adel Kelany reports three types of hoof prints:

1. Large bovid prints, 14 cm long and 5 cm wide

2. Medium-size hoof print, 8 cm × 12 cm and 7 cm deep, possibly from donkeys. These were the most common.

3. Smaller size prints, 5 cm × 6 cm, around 2 cm deep, possibly from goats.

The directions of the prints are a bit random and may reflect animals milling about or going to and from the Gate in the Wall of the Crow.

We have found footprints in the ruin surface or "mud mass" at the following places across the site:

- East end of the Chute, two human footprints in the mud mass near the end of the north wall of the Chute in Square 3.L34.

- At the far eastern end of Main Street East in Squares 4.L27–28 and near a north-south mudbrick wall marking the end of the street, animal footprints.

- In SFW, the Western Town, Squares 6.E-F-G7, and farther southwest, Squares 6.F4, 6.E2.

The tracks tell us that the surface of the ruins, as we find it, was exposed and wetted, most probably by rain, and then dried, preserving the prints before wind laid down the heavy blanket of clean sand.

We have actually witnessed the site in such a mushy condition, or close to it. On Tuesday, March 13, 2001, rain fell from midnight until we went to work at 7:00 AM. *Tafla* clay surfaces (such as the coatings on the troughs and benches in the Hypostyle Hall, or the plaster faces on walls and floors of the galleries) liquefied. We could smear the *tafla* surfaces with our fingers. (Why, therefore, was it so important for the inhabitants 4,500 years ago to coat interior and exterior surfaces with this clay?)

The rain soaked into sandy surfaces for a depth of 11 cm and pooled in lower parts of the site. Much more substantial rains and pools were required, over the long term, to leave the *tafla* and gravel layers that we found in Area SFNW. But early in the day, March 13, 2001, we could have certainly left our own tracks.

The WCGN Trenches

We did not know, as we looked at the compact surface north of the Gate late in the 2004 season, what might lie beneath. We did not have time to excavate the whole exposure, so we decided upon a few strategically placed trenches (fig. 1).

Trench A

We chose the location of Trench A, along the north sides of Squares 1.G33 and 1.G34 as far north as possible—while being on line with the Gate—to check if an ancient road or a structure continued northward from the Gate under the compact surface (fig. 31). Trench A was 1.50 m wide north-south, 8.60 m long east-west, and more than 1.80 m deep.

Trench B

Trench B extended farther northward from, and perpendicular to, Trench A. The purpose was to track the deposits under the Old Kingdom surface as far north as our exposure would allow. Trench B, on the eastern side of Square 1.H33, was 4.90 m long (north-south) and 1.50 m wide (east-west).

Trench C

Trench C was 1.70 m east-west and 0.95 m north-south across the southern end of the double mudbrick lines in the northeast part of Square 1.E35.

Trench D

Trench D was on the northern side of Square 1.E34 to check for the sequence under the compact surface closer to the Gate than Trench A. Trench D was 1 m wide, and 5 m long east-west, located 14 m to the north of the Gate and 9 m north of the 2001 square.

Kelany's team did not excavate the other trenches as deeply as Trench A, rather only as far as was necessary as to find the same or similar sequence and character of layers as we found in Trench A.

The sequence north of the Gate in the Wall of the Crow is remarkable for having none of the thick settlement deposits and architecture such as we find immediately on the south side of the Wall of the Crow. The layers to the north contain very little cultural material and no architecture under the compact surface. Trench A was our main reference section for the depositional sequence.

Kelany's team did a meticulous excavation of many lenses and layers, more than two dozen in Trench A alone. They carefully described each and every layer and assigned each layer its own feature number. They documented the layers in plans, section drawings, and photographs. Here we will "lump" these layers and describe the general character of the whole sequence.

The section in Trench A shows a top layer, 10 cm or less in thickness, of fine compact sand, then the compact surface of a layer of crushed marly limestone and *tafla* ranging from a few centimeters to 25 cm thick, probably generally within this range across the whole of our exposure in WCGN. The west end of Trench A cut through a patch of granite dust, 22 to 23 cm thick. Underneath the compact layer of crushed limestone and *tafla* is a laminated series of fine to coarse grainy sand with multiple surfaces, or dry lines interspersed with lenses of coarser gravelly sand that appear to have been sorted by water or wind. Lower in the sequence, there are large patches of dense, concentrated *tafla*, very fine and consistent, up to 16 cm thick. The lower layers contained large limestone pieces and desert chert cobbles.

Kelany took the trench down to a depth of more than 1.80 m to the water table at elevation 14.56 asl. (This is very close to the level of the water table in his trench in West Dump and to the level of the ground water in Lagoon 1). The sequence of coarse sand and chip layers continued lower in the excavation. The layers are very horizontal and contained quartz pebbles. The lowest layers were very coarse sand, up to 43 cm thick. Among large limestone pieces at the bottom, close to the water table, one was unusually large, triangular or trapezoidal in shape, 92 cm long, 18 cm thick, and 80 cm wide.

Our impression is that many of these layers are water-sorted or were spread by water. The water may have flowed out of the wadi and washed out across this site.

In summary, Trench A revealed a shallow occupation on a compact surface that extends along the north side of the Wall of the Crow from the Gate to the east end. We found only thin occupation deposits over the compact surface. It is possible that cultural deposits were washed or otherwise eroded from the surface. The two lines of mudbricks appear to have been eroded down to a thickness of a few millimeters. The compact surface itself is cultural. People spread that layer of crushed limestone and *tafla*, probably very intentionally, upon gritty sand, gravels, and *tafla* layers that wind and water lay down in a broad, open area.

A remarkable fact about Trench A was that its south section happened to fall exactly on the drill core hole that Serena Love carried out north of the Gate in 2002 (fig. 31). The south section neatly halved the drill hole, which was already filled with gray, sandy material, probably fallen in from the modern layers high above. The drill penetrated 1.50 m below the compact Old Kingdom surface. The core

Mark Lehner

Figure 31. WCGN operation. The profile of Trench A in the foreground shows sediments nearly devoid of cultural material. The hole running down the center is from a drill coring taken during the 2001 field season. View to the south.

drilling and Trench A offer a good opportunity to test drill core results against excavation.

Final Clearing North of the Wall of the Crow

We began working north of the wall of the Crow in the mode of salvage archaeology because of plans for the reportedly imminent building of a cement and steel mesh corridor parallel to the Wall of the Crow and somewhere close to it. To reiterate, the corridor was to allow mourners attending funerals to move from the town to the Muslim and Coptic Cemeteries. The corridor was planned to depart from an opening that would be made in the high security wall that was completed in 2002. This wall turns a corner, coming from the east toward the west, and then running north, just opposite the east end of the Wall of the Crow.

One possibility was that the corridor would exit an opening in the south face of the corner of the high security wall, jutting toward the Wall of the Crow. From here the corridor would turn west to run parallel to the Wall of the Crow as far as in front of the ancient Gate. Here the corridor might turn north to the Muslim Cemetery, with a path departing south to the Gate for the Christian funerals to proceed to the Coptic Cemetery, on the opposite side of the Wall of the Crow.

Our clearing this season in collaboration with the Giza Inspectorate opened a space from the Wall of the Crow northwards for 35 m, from the Gate to the east end of the Wall (modern tombs already encumber the north side of the Wall west of the Gate). This clearing left a section that dropped 4 m from the southern edge of the tourist bus parking lot. (The overburden rises at the west end of the section, in front of the Gate through the Crow Wall, to 7 m above the compact Old Kingdom surface). The clearing this season created a buffer between the Wall of the Crow and the planned corridor.

In the last week of May, Mohammed Musilhi came back for a week of work with the loader. He pushed the section through the overburden back another 5 m to the north, to about 40 m distant from the Wall of the Crow. Next, working from the top, he lowered the surface across an additional 5-m strip to the north down to just above the layer of ancient clean sand. The east end of this strip stops at the west face of the corner in the 2002 security wall, on line with the modern street just behind. This allows for the corridor, should it be built, to depart from the west face of the 2002 wall, which would keep clear the entire 35-m buffer that we gained through our work this season. The steel mesh corridor will hopefully not attach to the Gate of the Wall of the Crow. Rather, a gate in the cement corridor could control for the Christian funerals to pass across our buffer zone and through the ancient stone Gate.

References

Bruning, L.
2003   Data Structure Report for Operation WCE (Wall of the Crow East). Report on file, Ancient Egypt Research Associates, Inc. (AERA).

Foster, A.
2004   North Street Gate House: Summary of 2004 Excavation Season. Report on file, AERA.

Gesell, J., M. Kamel, Y. Kawae, M. Kincey, and T. Evans
2004   Data Structure Report of Soccer Field West (SFW). Report on file, AERA.

Kaiser, J.
2005   The Late Period Cemetery: Excavations and Findings, 2000–2005. Report on file, AERA.

Kelany, A.
2004   Data Structure Report of Excavations North of the Gate of the Wall of the Crow (WCGN) in 2004. Report on file, AERA.

Lehner, M.
1992   Giza. *The Oriental Institute 1990–1991 Annual Report*, ed. by W. H. Sumner, pp. 19–27. Chicago: The Oriental Institute.

1993   Giza. *The Oriental Institute 1991–1992 Annual Report*, ed by W. H. Sumner, pp. 56–67. Chicago: The Oriental Institute.

2001   Giza. T*he Oriental Institute 2000–2001 Annual Report*, ed. by G. Stein, pp. 46–68. Chicago: The Oriental Institute.

2002   The Pyramid Age Settlement of the Southern Mount at Giza. *Journal of the American Research Center in Egypt* 39: 27–74.

2003   The Giza Plateau Mapping Project. *The Oriental Institute 2002–2003 Annual Report*, ed. by G. Stein, pp. 64–69. Chicago: The Oriental Institute.

Lehner, M., M. Kamel, and A. Tavares
2006   *Giza Plateau Mapping Project, Season 2005, Preliminary Report*. Giza Occasional Papers 2. Boston: Ancient Egypt Research Associates.

Milward-Jones, A.
2004   Data Structure Report for EOG 4.F20–22 and 4.G20–22. Report on file, AERA.

Nicholson, P. T. and E. Peltenburg
2000   Egyptian Faience. In *Ancient Egyptian Materials and Technology*, ed. by Paul T. Nicholson and Ian Shaw, pp. 177–94. Cambridge: Cambridge University Press.

Redding, R.
2004   The Faunal Remains from Excavations at Area A, a Habitation Site Southeast of the Pyramids at Giza. Report on file, AERA.

Sharman, P.
2003   Excavations in WCS and WCG: GPMP Season 2001A, Feb.–May 2001. Draft Data Structure Report. Report on file, AERA.

Tonner, T.
2002   WCE-SE 2002 Excavation: Post-Occupation Deposits. Report on file, AERA.

The 2004 Team

Project Director
Mark Lehner

Assistant Director
John Nolan

Field Director
Mohsen Kamel

Assistant Field Director
Ana Tavares

Archaeobotanists
Mary Anne Murray (team leader)
Rainer Gerisch
Mennat-allah el-Dorry

Archaeozoologist
Richard Redding

Artifact Analysts
Meredith Brand
Marie-Astrid Calmettes

Artists
Johnny Karlsson
Marcia Gaylord

Archaeologists
Adel Kelany
Ali el Selhdar
Amira Hassan Abdallah
Angela Milward-Jones
Ann Foster
Ashraf Abd el-Aziz
Astrid Huser
Brian V. Hunt
Dan D. U. Hounsell
Emma Hancox
Fatma Hussein Mohammed Ali
Freya Sadarangani
Hala Said
Hanan Mahmoud Soliman
Hasan Mohamed Abd el-Razeq
Heba Hosni Attia
James Taylor
Justine Gesell
Lauren Bruning
Marie-Astrid Calmettes
Mark E. Kincey
Mohammed Abd el-Aziz
Shiamaa Abd el-Rahman
Tim Evans
Tobias Tonner
Yukinori Kawae

Conservator
Ed Johnson

Ceramicist
Anna Wodzińska

Sealings Analysts
John Nolan (team leader)
Ali Witsell
Hratch Papazian
Joshua R. Trampier

Database Manager
Tobias Tonner (designer and manager)

Osteo-archaeologists
Jessica Kaiser (team leader)
Johnny Karlsson
Tove Björk